LIFE
WITHOUT
FEAR

Joseph Wolpe, M.D.

with

David Wolpe

New Harbinger Publications, Inc.
5674 Shattuck Ave.
Oakland, CA 94609

An earlier version of this work was published as *Our Useless Fears*
(Boston: Houghton Mifflin, 1981).

A portion of chapter 3 was published in *The Practice of Behavior Therapy,*
by Joseph Wolpe, M.D. (Elmsford, N.Y.: Pergamon Press, 1973), and in *Handbook of
Behavioral Interventions,* edited by Alan Goldstein and Edna B. Foa (New York:
John Wiley & Sons, 1980).

To Stella

Contents

Preface

The striking success of behavior therapy has generated a great deal of interest, as shown by the appearance of many self-help books and the popularity of assertiveness training and stress management methods. However, the essential features of behavior therapy are poorly understood by the educated public and by many professionals in the mental health field. No clear and authoritative account has been available. This book is intended to provide that account.

For many years I had resisted the idea of writing a book for an audience outside the field of behavior therapy. The situation changed when my son David, a playwright, expressed interest in collaborating on such a book. We envisaged the writing process as follows: Armed with the general understanding of behavior therapy that he had gained over the years, David would use his special gift for expressing difficult ideas in a simple way to translate into nontechnical language the material that I would provide. But this did not work, and it became evident that the desired product could only be achieved by a true collaboration. The book eventually evolved from many discussions, with David often drawing me out on details that he needed to be able to convey the ideas. In intermittent meetings of varied length over a year, this collaboration resulted in a first draft of the book. We then, in further meetings, molded and refined it, idea by idea and sentence by sentence. This was a time-consuming but extraordinarily gratifying experience. It is good fortune for a father to be able to work constructively and harmoniously with his son.

We are thankful to Betty Jean Smith, who typed and organized innumerable drafts and repeatedly provided significant feedback. We are also grateful to David Harris, Jean-Claude van Itallie, and Stephen Lande for extensive and detailed criticisms; to Paul Latimer, Debora Phillips, Joseph Chaikin, and Allan Wolpe for their comments; and to Matthew McKay for constructive suggestions that led to significant enhancement of the final manuscript. Constantly involved with the book was Stella Wolpe, who provided ideas, criticism, and encouragement.

JOSEPH WOLPE, M.D.

I

Useful and Useless Fears

Introduction

If useless fears were short-lived, like the common cold or a sprained ankle, they could be endured and then forgotten. Unfortunately, they usually persist for years and often for life. That is why they and their consequences— depressions, obsessions, compulsions, headaches, sexual difficulties, and others—are a matter of so much concern to humanity. The centuries have seen an endless succession of treatments: prayer, the laying-on of hands, dreaming outside the temple walls, exorcisms, drugs, herbs, and a vast array of rituals, to say nothing of the psychotherapies of today. Among these psychotherapies, psychoanalysis continues to hold center stage in spite of its poor record of success in relieving human suffering.

I was myself for some years a supporter of the psychoanalytic position, even though as a medical student I had found Freud's theories colorful but incredible. My positive attitude started from an incident that took place toward the end of my medical internship at Johannesburg General Hospital in 1940. A freckled, ginger-haired 17-year-old girl named Hetty had been in the ward for six months, suffering from what seemed to be a form of St. Vitus' dance, a disease of the nervous system characterized by jerky movements. Hetty was unusual in that she made not only the characteristic jerks and twitches, but also sinuous, writhing, snakelike movements of her back, arms, and head. She had improved considerably after being treated with sedative drugs, but because of the writhing movements her doctors were not sure that their diagnosis was correct. One day she told me that she often dreamed she was swimming in a lake toward a man on a distant shore that she never reached. A psychoanalyst to whom I reported this dream suggested I try giving her the "obvious" interpretation that she had a desire for a "nice young man like her father." The next day I went into the ward and told Hetty that I could explain the meaning of her dream. She listened to my explanation without saying a word. I left the ward and crossed the passage to do some work in the next room. About ten minutes later a nurse burst in, shouting, "Doctor! Come and see what's happened to Hetty!" I rushed back to the ward and saw her in a convulsion of movements worse than she had ever had before. She remained in much the same state until my departure to another hospital two weeks later.

Even though the effects of the statement were disadvantageous to Hetty, they seemed to indicate an origin for her illness along psychoanalytic lines. There *had* been a clear change in her condition within minutes after I had presented her with the interpretation. It seemed plausible, therefore, that Hetty's illness had something to do with a "fixation" on her father. (I did not then consider the possibility that a young girl might be distressed at the suggestion that she was sexually interested in her father—and that nervous symptoms might be worsened by this distress, whether their cause was psychological or physical.)

I began to look with new interest at psychoanalysis, to read Freud's books, and to record my own dreams and free-associate to them—with results that were often intriguing. I found unexpected connections between names, people, and images that seemed to make sense and to support the Freudian view of things.

Later experiences raised doubts. In 1943 I enlisted in the South African Medical Corps, and soon afterward was stationed at a military hospital in Kimberley that received, among other cases, many soldiers with war neuroses from the battle areas in North Africa. The most favored treatment at that time was narcoanalysis, which calls for the injection of a "truth drug" into the patient's vein. Once in the woozy state the drug causes, the patient is encouraged by the therapist to talk about the battle experiences presumed to have set off the neurosis. The procedure is based on the psychoanalytic idea that bringing memories out into the consciousness ought to be beneficial. I was always elated to hear a soldier vividly narrating his battle experiences, for I took this to mean that the treatment was working. But after many weeks it was clear to me that, while many patients were somewhat improved, there were no marked or lasting changes. This was very disappointing, and, although narcoanalysis is not exactly psychoanalysis, it led me to question psychoanalysis as well. My skepticism was increased when I read A. Wohlgemuth's *Critical Examination of Psychoanalysis* and C. W. Valentine's study of children from birth until the age of 8, in which he was unable to find confirmation of Freud's theory of the psychosexual development of young children.[1]

This led me to consider other possibilities, the most straightforward of which was that useless fears and the neurotic phenomena that result from them may really be directly learned responses. And so, armed with the knowledge of the learning process as revealed by laboratory studies, I began to study the experimental neuroses—the persistent fear habits of animals described in Chapter IV. The method by which I finally succeeded in overcoming these animal fears was the starting point for the clinical treatment methods of modern behavior therapy. These methods have, fortunately, transformed the outlook for many people who suffer from useless fears and their consequences.

The Faces of Fear

Fear is a feeling we all have in certain situations. We know it when someone pulls a gun on us, when we're told our plane is going to make a crash landing, when a loud noise surprises us on a dark street at night, when the driver of our car does eighty miles an hour on a country lane. The feeling in each of these situations is basically the same, although according to the context, it varies in intensity and, to some extent, in quality. Different situations give overtones to feelings that lead us to use different words for what is always, at bottom, fear.

- A wife is *worried* about her husband driving through an ice storm at night.
- A man feels *guilty* about having lied to his girlfriend.
- An actor is *nervous* before going onstage.
- A man is too *embarrassed* to tell a woman that he feels affection for her.
- A businessman becomes *fearful* when he steps onto an airplane.
- A girl is *anxious* about the results of an examination.
- A child is *terrified* of the dark.
- A boy is *uneasy* in a train station as the man sitting across from him begins laughing senselessly.

These different words indicate real differences in the individual experiences. Nevertheless, central to them all is a single group of physiological events within our bodies that usually include rapid pulse rate, sweating palms, rapid breathing, raised blood pressure, and increased tension in the muscles. In this book we will use the words *fear* and *anxiety* interchangeably to apply to all these experiences.

The Origins of Fear

The fear situations in the list above have all, in one way or another, acquired their fear-arousing power through experience. They are learned fears. But where did fear come from in the first place?

The answer is that it was originally produced by pain. When a child is struck by his parents, he feels pain. If he were physiologically monitored at that moment, the group of responses mentioned above—sweaty palms, rapid pulse, and so on—would be detected. He may not experience fear, because the pain overrides it. But later, when his parent approaches him and raises an arm as if to strike him once again, the child will show that same physiological pattern—and this time he feels fear. In other words, the physiological responses have become *conditioned* to the sight of his parent's menacing gesture, and they are felt as fear.

The physiological reactions produced by pain do not depend on learning. They are innate reasons, "wired in" as part of the physical development of our nervous system. This pattern can also be produced in the child (without learning) by some other experiences: loud noises, falling, and conflict. It also has been noted that children become afraid of unfamiliar faces when they first become able to distinguish them from their parents'. Together with pain, these are the original sources of all fears. Whatever happens to be around when fear is aroused—things, people, words, sounds—anything seen or heard or felt, anything making an impact on the person—can become attached to the fear through learning.[2] It is *emotional learning,* the effect of which is that this thing or sound is by now able to arouse fear. And the newly learned fear, too, is attachable to other events in whose presence it occurs. In this way, fear spreads from one experience to another, link by link.

What Can Be Feared?

Almost anything can become a trigger to fear. Among the more common fears are those of:

public speaking	being alone
flying	blood
making mistakes	open wounds
failure	dentists
disapproval	injections
rejection	taking tests
angry people	police

Less common are fears of:

heights	deformed people
dogs	hospitals
spiders	darkness

One can see from the above lists that even situations that are in themselves utterly remote from any danger can become fear triggers. What danger, for example, can be read into the sight of the setting sun? Yet a man once came to me because, among other things, he was deeply upset each day by the late afternoon sun. He had no idea why, but on investigation, I found that his fear dated from a troubled romance he had had several months earlier. He was working then in an army camp in Arizona. Each evening, just after work, he would walk to a telephone booth to call his sweetheart. Their relationship was disintegrating, as she had become attracted to another man. During these conversations, he would argue and plead with her to come back to him, but to no avail. As he spoke, the red setting sun was visible in the enormous sky over the desert. Because that image was so vivid, it became a trigger to his disturbed feelings, and these could still be set off each evening at sunset if he was out of doors, even though the romance no longer mattered to him.

Distinguishing Between Useful and Useless Fears

Fears may be considered useful when they are aroused in circumstances where there is a real threat; useless fears are aroused when there is no such threat. The contrast is illustrated by the following example. If, walking through a park, I come upon a snarling tiger, the fear I feel is appropriate because there is real danger. But if, instead of a tiger, I see a small mouse and am terrified by that harmless creature, the fear is useless.

Fortunately for us, most of the fears we learn are appropriate and may promote helpful action. It is appropriate to fear an angry bully, a reckless driver, or a loved one's dangerous illness. We are also rightly afraid at the news of an approaching tornado or of a murderer at large, at feeling a pain in the chest that we know may indicate a heart condition, or at hearing that we are losing our savings on the stock market. If a man living in a ghetto is worried because he does not know where his next meal is coming from, and if he is afraid that the large rats that infest his house may attack his children, then his fears are not useless; they are realistic. His problem is not one for therapy; what needs to be changed is not his reaction to the situation, but the situation itself. Similarly, the unmarried daughter in a religious family has good reason to fear pregnancy, because her family may condemn or even disown her if she becomes pregnant. It is not her fear reaction that needs to be changed; it is her situation—in this case, perhaps through birth control. Such fears make sense because some real danger or disadvantage threatens.

Useful fears function largely as a signaling device, directing us to the presence of a danger to be dealt with. They prompt worthwhile action: to see a doctor for chest pain, to leave for home before the blizzard that is forecast, to slow down on the expressway, or to take whatever other protective action may be relevant. In any activity that presents a sequence of dangers, fear focuses our attention on the hazards of each moment. A mountaineer who is edging his way along a precipice two thousand feet high takes good care to see and feel where his next step will be; he is acutely aware of the crumbling rock, the frayed rope, the wind, and his foothold on the side of the mountain. His fear keeps him alert to whatever he needs to do in order not to fall. In long-term pursuits, too, low-level fear may benefit an individual, by leading him, for instance, to study diligently over the months and years to pass his examinations.

We call a fear useless when, instead of being helpful, it gets in the way. A fear of poor sexual performance may devastate a man's sex life, and a fear of being seen in the nude may seriously limit a woman's. Anxiety aroused in the work setting—caused, for example, by being watched while working—may impair one's productivity. Anxiety in social situations takes the pleasure out of them, may make it difficult for some people even to carry on a conversation, and in others causes stuttering or blushing. There is, in fact, no human activity that anxiety cannot impair. Many excellent golfers do poorly in competitions because being the focus of attention makes them anxious.

In some circumstances it is not the mere presence of fear but its *intensity* that determines whether it is or is not appropriate. A soldier may be so terrified of the bullets flying around him that he is unable to defend himself. The fear is certainly appropriate in the sense that no one would regard it as extraordinary or bizarre. Its magnitude, though, is a drawback, making it disadvantageous and placing it in the category of useless fear.

In another context, most people crossing a street at rush hour would feel slightly apprehensive; they would be careful, keep their eyes open for oncoming traffic, look both ways, cross with the light, and so on. Their appropriately low level of fear would help them to cope with the possible danger. But occasionally we find a person who is so afraid that he or she is quite unable to cross the street at all, or to whom the crossing is a torment.

Like everything else, useless fears must be seen in perspective. They do not all necessarily require treatment. A very large number of useless fears do not materially interfere in people's lives. This is the case when they are very mild, and especially if they are both mild and infrequent. A person may have a creepy feeling about spiders or fishmoths, or a vague disquiet on the top story next to a window, or when in a foreign country. If such a weak fear is the only one a person has, it is usually not worth treating.

Fear in Disguise

In addition to the distress that a useless fear directly causes and the damage it can do to a person's work and social and sex life, it may have other consequences that can obscure the fear itself. Among these consequences are obsessional thinking, compulsive cleanliness, asthma, tension headaches, stuttering, depression, and uncertainty about one's role in the world (the so-called existential neurosis). These reactions may dominate a person's life, and yet he may be quite unaware that fear has anything to do with them. Thus, when he comes to a therapist, he makes no mention of anxiety.

People who do not know much about behavior therapy tend to think that such cases are too subtle or ill-defined to be suitable for it. They believe that it is applicable only to clear-cut problems, like phobias. But a crucial function of behavior therapy is to tease out the factors that operate in every case. The case is thus given definition, no matter how diffuse it may have looked in the first place. Here are some examples:

> DALE, 39 years old, divorced, secretary at a university, had migraine attacks and became extremely fatigued under pressure. She also had pains in the abdomen. These symptoms had diminished somewhat after she had left her husband two years previously, but she could not understand why she still had any symptoms. She made no mention of fear.

> DENNIS, 46, an electrician, complained of being very easily upset emotionally, leading to constipation and headaches. He felt that his sex life had always been impaired by this. If he was upset in the evening, he would wake at night with his mouth dry and bitter. He did not mention anxiety.

> AMY, 36, a housewife, had been married for ten years. She and her husband were constantly bickering because she was overly sensitive. Her husband said, and she agreed, that she was very difficult to live with.

> LYDIA, 44, a social worker, complained of insomnia. It began after her husband had a heart attack twelve years before. During the last four years, she would lie awake most of the night, listening to his breathing, because his father had died in his sleep. At six in the morning he would leave, and then she would fall asleep until eight or nine.

> GREGORY, 45, a metal appraiser, married for two years, had a sexual fetish: he became sexually excited only if his wife was wearing high-heeled shoes. Further, he could have intercourse any time except bedtime, and usually he insisted in tying her ankles together. Except for her legs, which had to be bare, she had to be fully dressed, and there had to be a minimum of love play. Needless to say, this caused a good deal of tension between them.

> MAUDE, 22, a teacher of dancing, complained of bouts of depression. She had difficulty in coping with problems, and she resented those who could manage better. She complained of no anxiety, and she knew no rhyme or reason for her depression.

TONY, a 30-year-old physician, easily became extremely angry. He usually bottled up his anger. Instead of expressing it, he spoke sarcastically and occasionally threw things, including books, ashtrays, and the telephone.

None of these people complained of anxiety, or even seemed bothered by it. Yet all of them were completely cured when the true anxiety-related causes of their problems were determined and dealt with. Dale's migraines and abdominal pains disappeared when her oversensitivity to criticism was overcome. Dennis's dry and bitter mouth ceased to wake him when his undue worry about being disapproved of was eliminated. Amy and her husband were able to get along after she was helped to conquer her timidity through assertiveness training, and to quell fears of death and of the presence of groups of people, which were, in rather complex ways, related to her oversensitivity. Lydia's insomnia was found to be based on anxiety and was overcome by desensitizing her to death-related scenes. Gregory's sexual fetish responded to fifteen sessions of desensitization (see Chapter V); the emotion analysis showed that it was based on fears of poor sexual performance. Maude's emotional problems were solved when the timidity that was revealed was treated by assertiveness training. Assertiveness training, in addition to proving that he was not going crazy, as well as desensitization to half a dozen social fears (for example, that of being late), overcame Tony's excessive anger.

These examples are typical of the ways in which a great many problems are presented to psychotherapists. The underlying anxieties are there to be found and dealt with if one knows how to look for them, how to find the factors that trigger them, and what to do with the information once it has been obtained. Later we shall consider examples that show in detail how the depression or headache or other complaint may be related to useless anxiety, and how overcoming the anxiety habit is the way to recovery.

II

How People Develop
Useless Fears

A useless fear may be born in one moment, from a single experience, or it may develop over time, on the basis of a whole series of events. It becomes attached to a situation (1) when a fear is aroused in that situation, either directly or through conflict, or (2) as the result of misinformation.

Anyone can develop a useless fear. Such a fear does not indicate that a person is constitutionally inferior, that he is morally weak or mentally unstable. Fears are, however, more likely to develop in two kinds of people. The first is the highly emotional person. In a frightening situation, he or she will experience higher anxiety, and therefore more anxiety is likely to be attached to the situation. The second is an individual who, because of an early fearful experience, will be more vulnerable to the later development of severe fears arising from similar experiences. But contrary to popular belief, it is not necessary that the critical events occur in early childhood. They can take place at any age; they can spring up virtually anywhere, at any time, in connection with almost anything. A person's susceptibility is not affected by how intelligent or athletic or capable he or she is.

Fears Caused by a Single Event

A habit of useless fear frequently develops on the basis of a single intense fear experience. Some of the most striking examples relate to the onset of war neuroses. A corporal kneels with his platoon in a cornfield, firing a machine gun. All of a sudden his neighbor is disemboweled by a piece of shrapnel and, screaming in agony, dies in a few minutes. The corporal is panic-stricken and has an almost irresistible urge to get away. The fear he feels is later found to have become attached to everything in that environment—all the sights and sounds and smells of the battlefield. Later encounters with such things, either in reality or through words or pictures, produce fear. If the sound of the machine gun was particularly prominent at the crucial time, it is likely to become an especially strong trigger to fear; and similar sounds—a motorcycle ascending a hill, for example—will also elicit fear, but at a lower intensity, by *generalization* (see Chapter III).

Whatever is acting most strongly on the person at the time the fear is aroused, whatever is at his center of attention, will become most strongly attached to the fear. In the above example, it was the sound of the machine gun. The sight of blood, the drizzly rain, the sound of the screams, the smell of explosives were less strongly fear-connected because they happened not to be at the center of attention at the critical time.

In civilian life, too, fears are often caused by a single event.

SHARON, driving to the supermarket, was stopped at a red light. As the light turned green, she proceeded into the intersection, but was hit by a truck that had run the red light on the road she was crossing. She was not seriously injured but was terrified to see the truck bearing down on the side of her car the instant before it hit. From this moment, she had a fear of automobiles (and trucks) approaching from the side. She had no fear of oncoming traffic, but if she had to make a left turn so that traffic approaching was momentarily on the right side, she would become highly anxious, even if the approaching car was a full mile away.

JAMES, 32 years old, came for treatment because of an intense fear of traveling in or even being inside automobiles. This started from a single incident that had taken place four years previously. He had stopped his Volkswagen at a red light in a small town. A sudden impact from behind had thrown him forward, causing his forehead to strike the windshield. The only physical injury was a small cut on his head. James had not lost consciousness, but a surge of panic had swept over him, brought on by the thought "I am about to die." The fear became connected to the car's interior and spread to all car interiors; he had during these four years been unable to enter a car without great anxiety. Driving was out of the question.

HENRY, aged 40, belonged to a cave-exploration club. During an expedition to a labyrinth of caves, while he was deep underground and separated from his companions, a gust of wind blew out his light. He had no matches and was beset by a feeling of being entombed forever. He panicked. From then on, he had a fear not only of caves, but of any situation in which he felt confined: for example, traveling in an airplane, driving through a tunnel, riding on a train, or even lying in a tightly made bed.

One of the most common fears is that of speaking in public, or, more broadly, of being the center of attention. Often this fear originates in a single event.

AUDREY, a 21-year-old woman, described how her fear began when she was 12. She was standing in front of the class, reading from a history book, when she mispronounced a word. The class laughed jeeringly, and she felt deeply humiliated. From this time on, she was afraid to speak up in class and had great anxiety when she did. She was also anxious henceforward in social situations, especially if she had to tell a story or do anything else that drew attention to her.

Some very severe and disabling fears can be dated from a single experience.

STANLEY, a 52-year-old industrial consultant, had, since the age of 36, been crippled by a fear of being away from his home (a fear known as agoraphobia). To this he had adjusted by moving to an apartment one block from his office, but he could not walk even that distance without becoming very anxious. His work, too, was disrupted.

The story that unfolded was that twenty years earlier his wife, whom he dearly loved, had died of lung cancer, and he had watched her literally suffocate to death. Gradually he had gotten over the trauma of that experience, and after a year or so began to form relationships with women. Three years later, his trouble started. At that time he had a steady girlfriend, who would often spend the night at his apartment. One night, after an orgasm, she began breathing as though with difficulty and making movements that reminded him of his wife at the time when she was choking. Becoming increasingly anxious, he told his girlfriend he had to take her home immediately. In the car, Stanley began to notice that *he* was having trouble breathing, which worsened until he felt he was choking, and he panicked. He dropped the woman at a taxi stand and drove home immediately. With that experience, his fear of being away from home began, and later generated a group of satellite fears, including a fear of losing his mental stability, of meetings or parties (crowds), unfamiliar places, being alone in a car, and dead animals.

Fears Developing From Multiple Events

Equally common are useless fears that have gradually grown in strength as a result of fear arousals in many situations that are basically similar.

Agoraphobia arose out of a single experience in Stanley's case, but it sometimes develops gradually.

JOYCE, aged 30, had an initial brush with anxiety that left her with only a moderate aftermath of useless fear, but it was the beginning of a progressive build-up. Like Stanley, she dated her neurosis to a surge of anxiety while driving, when she partially blacked out on a highway. She swerved out of the way of oncoming traffic and guided her car onto the soft shoulder of the road, where she stopped. Dizziness and a feeling of faintness lasted about thirty minutes, during and after which she felt very anxious. Joyce resumed driving when these sensations stopped. During the half-hour drive home, the anxiety gradually subsided.

She avoided driving for a week. But now, when driving Joyce was nervous alone in the car or when she remembered blacking out or had any sensations at all suggestive of faintness. Each time she had this thought while driving, the anxiety level increased. It was further increased by two additional actual blackouts. After a few weeks, she began to realize that she was having attacks of anxiety without any apparent reason, and in a variety of situations—elevators, crowds, large department stores. The common element that I noted in these situations was that they all brought on a feeling of isolation, of being cut off.

In some cases there is clear evidence of one or more sensitizing experiences that may have taken place a long time earlier, perhaps in early childhood.

CHARLES, 58, a clothing designer, had a feeling of being lost in any unfamiliar place. It had begun when he was a child and then was suddenly made much worse in later life. When he was 6 years old and living in New York City, he accompanied a friend, who was going on vacation, to the train station. On the way home, he got lost, became confused, and began crying, and was eventually rescued by a policeman. Later, when he was 12 years old, he went to watch the New Year's Eve festivities at Time Square and had a strong feeling of being lost, along with a sense that he was unable to escape.

From then on, he felt uneasy in unfamiliar places and in crowds, but his anxiety was not sufficiently strong to disrupt his life. This changed when, a month before he came to see me, he made a business trip to London. After about an hour of standing in a hotel lobby with people whom he had just met, he had an overwhelming feeling of being lost—he looked around and realized that the place and the people were completely unfamiliar to him. He wanted to run out but excused himself and walked across the street to a park. After about ten minutes, the anxiety waned and he returned to the group. But he remained uneasy for the rest of the trip, and since that time any strange place caused the same panicky feeling.

Similarly, fears of public speaking or of being the center of attention may build up gradually instead of occurring in a "single shot." One finds most commonly a history of disturbing classroom situations, each producing a higher level of fearfulness. But the presensitization—the early fear experience that makes one more vulnerable to a similar later fear experience—need not be in *early* childhood.

ARLINE, aged 35, a registered nurse, in the past year had had a severe fear of public speaking, even to very small groups. A mild version of this fear had begun when she was 9 years old. Her father, who was the principal of her elementary school, would often put her on display in front of adults to read or recite poetry. On one occasion, while reciting in front of the school board, Arline forgot her lines. A murmur went through the group. She became confused, recited the wrong lines, and was greatly embarrassed, yet she recovered enough to plow on and finish the recitation. After this, she was consistently afraid of performing in public, though she often did speak in front of the class. Because the fear was not severe, Arline did not seek therapy.

About a year before I saw her, she had accompanied her husband, a business executive, to a convention in a distant city. She had gone reluctantly, fearing that she would be the center of attention with him. Despite his assurance that this would not happen, it did, and an enormous amount of anxiety was aroused in her. After this, Arline was afraid to talk even to small groups or on the telephone. Since she frequently needed to give reports to the doctors and nurses at the hospital where she worked, this was a terrible disadvantage, and she found it agonizing.

Many social fears—such as the fear of criticism or disapproval or of "doing the wrong thing"—develop through a long series of distressing experiences. A common story is of repeated chastisement by a parent who could never be pleased. It is scarcely surprising that, with a history of this kind, a child becomes fearful not only of that parent, but also of authority figures and perhaps a considerable range of other human beings. The degree of anxiety created by different people will be related to their similarity to the parent in terms of such factors as age, authoritativeness, facial and bodily features, gestures, and demeanor. Such a history often lies behind a person's general shyness, timidity, and lack of self-confidence.

Fears Developing From Conflict

Everyone knows that having to make a difficult decision can produce a good deal of emotional tension. The decisions, or conflicts, in daily life usually do no lasting harm, because they are quite quickly resolved. A man may be undecided about whether to sell his investments in the stock exchange, whether to visit relatives on a vacation (and which relatives), which of several cars to buy. He may be somewhat tense as he attempts to make the best decision in each case, but he does not become frantic. Much more severe tension can be produced by long-lasting conflicts involving major aspects of a person's life, such as what profession to choose. If the competing impulses are both strong and equally balanced, the person may be unable to make a decision.

The commonest conflict of this kind is found in certain women who are trapped in relationships they do not want. These women experience a rising level of continuous anxiety that comes from several sources; the anxiety may become connected to other situations, such as being away from home.

Fears Based on Misinformation

As we grow up we are told, most often by parents and teachers, about the dangers of a variety of things—dogs that growl, bees that sting, accepting rides from strangers, crossing an interstate highway, and so on. We come to think of all these things as "dangerous," and our emotional response to them is, in differing degrees, fear. After we learn what is meant when something is called dangerous, we may hear from someone that, for example, frogs are dangerous. If we believe him, frogs are now included in the class of things that we think of and react to as dangerous. We then fear frogs and try to avoid them, even though they are harmless.

> CHARLOTTE, a 21-year-old college student, had a wide range of social fears. She was unable to stand up for herself in practically any situation. She almost always felt guilty and apologetic. She was often depressed. For the past two years, she had taken to pulling out her eyelashes and eyebrows. She said the activity provided some relief from her misery. Her social fears, and the bizarre habit that emerged from them, had their origin in information conveyed to her by her governess when she was 4 years old. When she was naughty her governess threatened to turn her into bread. This terrified the child, and when the governess finally left to get married, she told Charlotte that she was doing so because the children who she had looked after were evil. These statements had initiated Charlotte's habit of feeling guilty.

In a similar way, people develop fears of masturbation because they have been told that it will injure their health. Many a young woman becomes afraid of sexual arousal because her mother tells her that it is disgusting and filthy or because she has gathered from religious teaching that feeling sexually aroused by any man who is not her husband is a "mortal sin" that will lead to eternal damnation.

Fears based on wrong information may also be transmitted by another person without the use of words. I once saw a woman with a fear of insects who told me that her two sisters had the same fear. All of them had repeatedly seen their mother react with terror to bugs of any kind and had wrongly inferred that every bug was dangerous.

> LISA, a 35-year-old pottery instructor, had been suffering greatly for more than ten years, during which she had continuously been in psychoanalysis. She was almost constantly depressed and had frequent temper tantrums, which were sometimes violent. Although she had never had an orgasm during sexual intercourse, she was able to masturbate to orgasm by squeezing her thighs together, but not in the presence of her husband. She had been very much discouraged by her therapist's statements that she was incapable of normal sexual function because her problems were so deep-rooted. In accepting this information, she had come to feel that she was irremediably inferior to other women.
>
> During my first few sessions with her, it became evident to me that this idea was the source of her depression. Moreover, the cause of her sexual difficulties was her fear of trusting people, a fear that arose from the way her father had behaved toward her. He had often and unexpectedly taken action behind her back. For instance, when she was 12, she had a pet dog that she loved dearly. One day while she was at school, her father decided that he disliked it and had it killed. Her inability to trust people was now at the root of her sexual problems. To have an orgasm in the presence of another person would be a kind of abandonment to that person, a self-exposure she could not risk.
>
> As soon as it became clear to her that her difficulties were based on a fear that could and would be overcome, the notion of her permanent inferiority was dispelled, and she experienced immediate and profound emotional relief. Her depression went away and did not return. She cooperated fully in the further steps that were needed to overcome her fear of trusting people and to achieve orgasms during intercourse. Her recovery has now lasted for nine years.

Fear and Memory

Although assertions are often made to the contrary, I have found, on careful questioning, that the events associated with the beginning of a fear are remembered in over 75 percent of cases. Such recall is particularly common when the fear started from a single event.

It is, however, interesting that so often, though the fear remains, the memory of the causal event disappears. This naturally happens when the fear has begun very early in life, as in the famous case of Little Albert,[1] who, at the age of 11 months, developed a fear of furry objects. But it can also happen much later, when long-term memory is well established. The fear habit belongs to the emotional nervous system, which is more primitive than the system that serves habits of thought (memories). Therefore, the memory may vanish, but the fear learned at the time does not. Thus, while it is always interesting and sometimes helpful to know when and how a fear began, it is not essential; what is essential is to gain a clear and precise picture of the triggers of the fear as it exists *now,* and the ways in which it interferes in the individual's life, regardless of how it might have come about. This issue is discussed more fully in Chapter X.

How Fear Spreads

We saw above how the range of fears can be increased by information that adds new things to one's mental category of what is "dangerous." And when fear is directly aroused in a given setting, things that are present at the time may become fear-connected. Now these newly feared things may also act as "carriers," spreading the fear to still other aspects of the environment. For example, Nancy, 33, with a fear of crowds, would go to the movies only in the daytime, when few people were present. One afternoon the movie house suddenly filled with students, sending her into a panic. After that she was afraid not only of crowds, but of movie houses, of restaurants, and churches—of any public building, even when it was empty.

Here is a case in which fear spread in several different ways.

THIRTY-TWO-YEAR-OLD JENNY often received harsh criticism from her husband, and began to dread his coming home from work. She did not pay much attention to her feelings, but worked instead to improve herself so that she would silence his criticisms. Still, she became gradually more tense when the time approached for him to arrive home, and became increasingly aware of physical symptoms. Her heart raced, she felt faint and lightheaded, and her hands became clammy. Never, though, did she connect these sensations with her husband. The symptoms frightened her, and when her doctor's prescribed medications did not help, she began to think she was "falling apart."

When her husband left for a week-long business trip, Jenny went to stay with her parents, and toward the end of the week visited a friend who was having a "nervous breakdown." Her friend looked exhausted and haggard, and Jenny asked herself whether the same thing was happening to her. Dwelling on this idea, she became intensely anxious and remained so during the last two days at her parents' house. When she returned home, she immediately began to improve. But she could not visit her parents' house again because it had become a trigger to her intense fear.

Jenny's fear, then, had spread in this way: her fear response to the criticisms from her husband gave rise to symptoms that included lightheadedness. These symptoms increased her anxiety, which was intensified still further when she visited her friend, since she connected her lightheadedness with the idea of having a "nervous breakdown." Her preoccupation with this idea caused a continuous high level of anxiety while she was at her parents' house. The final link in the chain was that she came to be afraid of visiting their house because of the anxiety that had become associated with it.

In all of the above examples, an individual finds himself reacting with fear under particular circumstances: in a car or away from home, as he thinks a certain thought or experiences bodily sensations; in front of a group of people, and so on. Whenever he subsequently finds himself in those circumstances, he has the same fear reaction. In other words, he has developed a *habitual* fear response, or fear habit. In the next chapter, we look at habits—what they are and how they work—and at fear habits in particular.

III

Habits and a Special Feature of Fear

Behavior therapy originated in a field of psychological research previously ignored by psychotherapists: the study of the laws of ordinary behavior and learning. Consequently, the vocabulary of this field is the basic vocabulary of behavior therapy. One of the most important words in this vocabulary is *habit*. It is related to, and includes, what we normally think of as a habit, but its meaning in behavior therapy is both wider and more specific.

A habit is a set of responses that is consistently triggered by the same circumstances. These responses are of three kinds: movement, feeling, and thought.

Most habits weaken and disappear when they do not serve the interests of the individual. Fear habits are a remarkable exception. In order to understand what makes them different, we must first examine briefly the features of habits, how they are formed, and how they are broken. We will consider the three kinds of responses separately (although they are almost always intertwined), beginning with movement (motor) habits, since these are familiar to everyone.

Habits of Movement

Many habits are small, fairly insignificant acts that we rarely notice. For example, a man has habits of stroking his chin when he is studying, of doodling with a pen while making a phone call, and of pursing his lips before answering a question. And he has a multitude of more complex habits, like cleaning up the bedroom before going out, stopping at a bar on the way home, watching the seven o'clock news, and reading a book at night before going to sleep.

Habits make a person's behavior predictable, but they can be interfered with. A woman usually goes to the toilet when she feels that her bladder is full, but not when the feeling arises in church in the middle of the sermon. A man who usually eats a large dinner loses his appetite when he learns that he may lose his job. I automatically doodle when I am on the telephone only if I have a pen and paper in front of me: the absence of paper prevents the activity. Similarly, I habitually wipe my shoes when I enter a house, but not if there is no doormat.

We have all developed thousands of movement habits, ranging from simple ones like those above to such amazingly complex skills as typing, piano-playing, and performing open-heart surgery. Each of these activities consists of intricate chains of habitual movements. Each includes an awareness of the changing scene, but some require less thought than others. The typist, for example, gets the paper, fits it into the machine, turns the cartridge, sets the margins, and then makes remarkably precise movements with his fingers—movements he has learned. He hits the keys in a strict order, one after another, determined by the words he is typing; depending on what he sees on the page, he may continue or go back and make corrections. This is the complex set of habits we call "typing." It has its parallel in countless others—driving a car, catching a baseball, sharpening a pencil, eating. There is a habit chain unique to each one of these activities, and each is self-contained in the sense that it does not overflow into the others.

Emotional Habits

We consistently have the same *emotional* responses to the same situations. Though we do not ordinarily refer to these as habits, they fit perfectly into the definition of habit given at the start of this chapter.

Emotions depend on activity of the *autonomic nervous system,* which controls the functions of our internal organs—for example, the heartbeat, intestinal contractions, and the activity of sweat glands. These functions are not, in the ordinary course of events, under our conscious control. Various combinations of autonomic responses are the physiological bases of the emotions that we feel and name: fear, anger, joy, disgust, surprise, being in love with a person, feeling friendly to another, disliking a third. We feel emotional change when something—a smile, a kiss, a gruesome sight—brings about a change in our autonomic nervous system.

The emotional response to a particular occurrence depends on previous learning. If the scent of musk oil has accompanied the romantic feelings aroused in me during candlelit dinners overlooking a lake in Switzerland, then that perfume in another place is likely to arouse the same romantic feelings. Similarly, earlier learning determines that a certain person's smile arouses a feeling of pleasure in me and his frown a feeling of dread. Sometimes, contradictory feelings are simultaneously aroused. I once saw an exquisitely crafted Grecian urn, but did not buy it because of a pattern near the top that resembled a swastika. The presence of that figure would have spoiled my enjoyment of the urn: I had one feeling, admiration, toward the line and elegance of the artwork and another, revulsion, because of what I had come to associate with the crooked cross.

Thinking Habits

Habits of thought are another category of behavior that we do not customarily call habits (or, for that matter, behavior). Yet certain thoughts are elicited as reliably as movements. The meanings and pronunciations of words exemplify this: we use words and pronounce them in much the same way from day to day. For example, the word *circle* arouses in us the image of a particular shape. Opinions of various kinds—indeed, many of our expressed attitudes—are also fairly clear-cut habits of thought. An individual consistently expresses his point of view when the question of, say, arms control is raised. It is this consistency that makes us call him a "liberal" if he has one set of expressed views and a "conservative" if he has another. One's opinions, like one's feelings, however, may be changed by new experience. With new information, a person's habit of thought is replaced or modified—he "changes his mind."

Thinking habits like those mentioned involve the association of a word with an image, or of a group of expressed ideas in response to a certain political issue. But there are other kinds of learning in which what is learned is not a simple association, but skills and ways of thinking. This is apparent in the learning of language, which Ludwig Wittgenstein likened to the learning of a game.[1] A person may learn to play bridge by watching others play. When he has learned it, however, he will not be confined to the bids and strategies that he has seen others make; he will also be able to originate his own. He has not memorized a particular set of moves, but from those which he has observed he has learned rules that enable him to act appropriately in new situations. Similarly, with speech one learns the rules from experience with a limited sample and becomes a kind of "creative participant," extending the use of language to meet the needs of each situation one encounters.[2]

In different individuals, different trains of thought may stem from the same situation, reflecting different learned ways of thinking. At a football game, one person may dwell exclusively on football strategy, trying to make sense of possible alternatives; to decide, for example, whether the quarterback should call a pass play at a particular moment in the game. Another person's response to the game is to see it symbolically, as a "war substitute," as a way of fighting without people actually killing each other.

Some therapies have given great emphasis to symbols and have assumed that they are, in fact, the key to a great many psychological problems. It is true that some fears—although a very small number—do have a symbolic role. An example is the case entitled "The Spider Was Mother," in Chapter IX.

Although the three kinds of habits—of movement, emotion, and thought—have been described separately, it is worth repeating that they occur in combination in virtually every human activity. For example, when driving a car, one has a succession of interrelated thoughts, feelings, and movements, mostly triggered by things that one sees and hears en route.

Interactions Between Responses

In the foregoing pages we have seen instances of the interaction of different habits—my conflict over the Greek vase, for example. In other instances, habit tendencies act in the *same* direction: a carpenter may be motivated *both* by his enjoyment of his craft *and* by the prospect of earning money.

But competitive interactions have the greater interest to us because of their role in therapy, as will be seen later. Responses are frequently in competition, and if, on a particular occasion, one response is stronger than a second, it will dominate and inhibit the second. If, on another occasion, the second response is the stronger, the first will be inhibited. If a young man is deeply upset by his poor grades, an evening with his girlfriend may be ruined. But if he is less upset, his feelings toward her and the pleasures of the evening may overcome his unhappiness. This relationship between responses was first noted by the British physiologist Sir Charles Sherrington, who labeled it *reciprocal inhibition*.[3] (Perhaps a more comprehensible term is *mutual inhibition*.)

Mutual inhibition is also readily demonstrated in movements. When the arm is bent, the excitation (tensing) of the biceps is accompanied by inhibition (relaxing) of the muscles behind the arm, and the opposite happens when the arm is straightened. If you try to straighten your knee against resistance, you will be able to tell, by pressing your hand on your thigh, that the muscles in the front of it are strongly contracted, and that the hamstring muscles at its back are very relaxed. A kind of "anti-response" has occurred in the hamstrings, making them actually more relaxed than they were when the leg was at rest. The functional value of this response is that it enables the leg to move forward more freely. In complex coordinated acts such as walking, there are alternations of excitations and their mutual inhibitions.

Mutual inhibition between emotional reactions has been clearly established by laboratory research.[4] Our awareness of these interactions among our own emotions is in keeping with this. Laughter is inhibited by sadness, anger, or anxiety, and can, in turn, inhibit them. (At times, of course, we have mixed feelings. Anger may be interfused with sadness or pity. When this happens, there is inhibition of some elements of the autonomic responses concerned and facilitation of others.)

The Physical Basis of Habits

It helps to understand why habits are so lasting if one realizes that they depend on pathways, established by learning, in the nervous system. Neurons (individual nerve cells) make up these pathways. A neuron becomes activated when another neuron excites it. This happens only when the meeting point between the two has the capacity to conduct impulses from one to the other. Conducive capacity comes about as the result of learning. A meeting point that has become conductive is called a *synapse*. The conductive capacity of a synapse is increased by further learning. Because *particular* sequences of neurons are connected to each other by synapses, the excitation aroused by a particular stimulus leads to a *particular* response. Of course, any human activity involves the excitation of thousands of neurons in concert.

How Habits Are Formed

The formation of habits depends on the establishment of new pathways in the nervous system. As these pathways are formed, the individual learns to respond in new ways to the world around him. It has been directly demonstrated in animal experiments that learning is correlated with the establishment of new connections between different parts of the brain.[5] For example, when an animal learns to raise its leg in response to a sound, a connection is made in the brain between certain hearing elements and leg-raising elements. If a man sees a stranger, he may have no appreciable reaction. If the stranger is an attractive woman, his response may be somewhat stronger. If he goes on to develop a relationship with that woman, he comes to feel deeply about her, and he will then respond strongly to her when he sees her. He has developed a response where no response (or a weak one) existed previously. In the nervous system, path-ways have been developed between the sight of the woman and these responses.

In the same way, if the mother of an infant consistently holds him in a certain position during feeding, the sensations of that position will, after a time, become triggers to salivation and the other responses of feeding. This means that these responses will then occur in the child when he or she is held in that position, even when no food is present. Other things that are present, such as the feeding bottle, can also acquire the power to trigger these responses.

Music-lovers go to concerts: they buy the tickets, they get dressed for the evening, make their way to the concert hall and to their seats, and they respond in various ways to the music. If they enjoy the music, it makes worthwhile the sequence of behaviors that they performed in order to be able to hear it.

For the baby, the eating of food is the final event in the sequence; for the music-lovers, it is hearing the music. These events provide a reward. Many experiments have shown that reward is the "cement" of learning. It is reward or its absence that determines whether a habit will be strength-ened or weakened. An animal in a simple maze will develop a left-turn habit if he always finds food at the end of a passage on the left; the habit will wane and die if the experimenter stops putting food in that place. If the musicians play out of key, or the concert is far below expectations, the reward is removed, and the audience's desire to hear these musicians again is diminished.

There are many kinds of rewards. Money is the reward we most readily think of in our society. Some of the most important rewards, though, are social; that is, they come from the behavior of other people. Social rewards are of many kinds. Obvious examples are praise, affec-tion, and sexual satisfaction. Less obvious ones are attention, smiles, and nods. Sometimes even adverse attention is rewarding, as seen in the child who persists in throwing tantrums even though he is punished for them—if that is the only way he can get attention.

Rewards that are still more subtle are in the satisfying of curiosity, in pleasant sensations of all kinds—the warmth of human flesh, the blue of the sky, musical sounds, and even "ordinary" experiences.

> Wet roofs, beneath the lamp-light; the strong crust
> Of friendly bread; and many-tasting food;
> Rainbows; and the blue bitter smoke of wood;
> And radiant raindrops couching in cool flowers;
> And flowers themselves, that sway through sunny hours.
> Then, the cool kindliness of sheets, that soon
> Smooth away trouble; and the rough male kiss
> Of blankets; grainy wood; live hair that is

Shining and free; blue-massing clouds; the keen
Unpassioned beauty of a great machine;
The benison of hot water; furs to touch;
The good smell of old clothes; and other such — [6]

The existence of so many sources of reward is what makes possible the wealth of our habits.

The scope of all learning is greatly extended by the phenomenon known as *generalization*. When a person has learned to respond to a particular event — whether it is a sound, an object, or a complex state of affairs — she or he will tend to make similar responses to similar events. This happens because every act of learning implies the attachment of a response not merely to that particular event, but to a *whole class of similar events*. The strength of a generalized response will depend on the *degree of similarity* between the generalized event and the original. For example, if a dog has been repeatedly fed at the appearance of a white disc, he will show excitement at its appearance, but less to a light gray disc, and less still to discs of darker and darker shades of gray. The "dimensions" of generalization can be of many kinds, including size, shape, position, loudness, brightness. Generalization is used in programs for overcoming useless fears, as we shall see in the chapters on treatment.

The Breaking of Habits

When a habit is eliminated or weakened, the process is called *extinction*. In the usual context in which it is studied, extinction is brought about by the withdrawing of the rewards that have established and maintained the habit. When I repeatedly find a favorite coffee shop shut and in darkness, my tendency to go there is progressively weakened. There have been many theories about how extinction works, but there is little doubt that competition from other responses (referred to above as reciprocal or mutual inhibition) has a major role. Apparently, when the reward does not arrive, the individual becomes frustrated, and the resulting responses weaken the previously rewarded one. [7] For example, an animal that has previously been rewarded for pressing a pedal but no longer receives food for this activity, makes other responses: he may sniff around the cage, run around in circles, try to bite the pedal, and so forth. These varied new motor responses compete with the old one — the pedal-pressing — and thus weaken the pedal-pressing habit.

The preceding example illustrates a general rule. When a response to a situation has become habitual, and a new (different) response to that situation is aroused, the habitual response is inhibited and weakened. This first became apparent in experiments on the process of forgetting, which was formerly assumed to be simply a matter of an impression fading as time passed. The fading theory finally fell from grace after a significant experiment on the forgetting of nonsense syllables.[8] The subjects each learned on several occasions lists of ten nonsense syllables (for examples, baf, yib, sev) until they had memorized them perfectly. Then on different occasions they were either kept awake or allowed to sleep for specified periods before being tested for recall. It was found that retention was far superior in those who slept than in the subjects who engaged in normal waking activities. Clearly, sleep preserved the learned associations, but the day's experience weakened them.

Later experiments showed that *forgetting occurs when the cues to particular images arise in the presence of new images.* The new images compete with the original ones and so weaken the latter's bond with the cues. During the time I lived in England, "the Island" always meant to me the Isle of Wight. After living for many years in Philadelphia, I find that it has come to mean Long Beach Island. The original image has been totally blotted out by the repeated occurrence of the newer experience in relation to the word *island.* By contrast, "Green Park" still evokes the English image, because there has been no competition with the park so named in London.

How Fear Habits Are Different

We are now in a position to see why strong anxiety response habits, once established, are so exceedingly persistent. The corporal with the fear of machine-gun-like sounds (discussed in Chapter II) goes on having that fear indefinitely, even though there is never a repetition of the terrifying experience from which it started. Why is that different from the pedal-pressing of the rat, which subsides when the food is no longer delivered? Something must account for the difference. That "something" has already been mentioned: it is the occurrence of competing responses. Other movement responses compete with the unrewarded pedal-pressing and thus weaken it. New experiences in relation to the word *island* competed with my former association with that word and thus weakened it. In the case of fear, *no such competing response occurs.* The corporal hears the machine-gun-like sounds and he feels fear. No feelings are aroused in him at the same time that can compete with the fear.

In order for a fear habit to be weakened, a competing response must occur together with it. Fortunately, this often does happen in life, quite by chance, which accounts for the fact that a good many useless fears "fade away" without formal treatment, especially if they were weak to begin with. When my older son was 3 years old, he began to be very much afraid of thunder, and cried and trembled each time a thunderstorm began. We were living at the time in Johannesburg, where in summer thunderstorms are frequent. Over a period of weeks, his fear became worse and worse.

My wife handled it in her own way. When a storm began, she would pick him up and rock him gently, singing, "Listen to the thunder, bringing lovely rain," to a tune she made up. In the course of four or five more thunderstorms, his fear melted away, and he no longer had to be picked up when there was one.

Countless mothers similarly reduce the fears of their children by soothing and calming. During World War II it was found that children who were alone when they experienced bombing raids were much more afraid of the sounds than children whose parents were present to comfort them. (This indicates the possibility of using competing emotions as a *preventive* measure. The prospects for preventive behavior therapy will be referred to again in Chapter X.)

Examples of the weakening of fears are also common in adult life. A medical student found that when the time came for him to do surgery, he was queasy at the sight of the blood and internal organs of the surgical patients. So he stood back a good distance from the table when observing an operation; this made it easier for him to bear. At the same time, he began to feel more and more interested in the surgical procedures. In order to be better able to see what was happening, day by day he gradually advanced closer and closer to the table. After a few days he was totally absorbed in what he was seeing, and the fear was gone.

Another example of such inadvertent weakening of fears is found in the relationship between therapist and patient, which automatically calls forth from many patients emotional responses that compete with their fears. This is the apparent reason that *all* psychotherapies have a fairly large number of successes.

Emotional competition seems to be needed to overcome not only fear, but all emotional habits. An obvious example is the persistence of unrequited love. A man may be unable for months or years to "accept emotionally" that the woman he loves no longer loves him; in other words, his emotional habit remains unchanged. He understands intellectually that the relationship is at an end. But the thought does not compete with the emotional response, so he continues to be in love, and he feels desolate over his loss. Only emotional competition can change the emotion.[9]

The behavior therapist deliberately uses competing responses to overcome useless fears. How this is done is described in the next three chapters.

IV

Animal Experiments That Solved the Fear Problem

Studies of severe fears produced in animals led to a way of overcoming the persistence of fear habits. These studies revealed crucial facts about the nature of useless fear, and the treatment methods used for animals provided a model for therapy of useless fears in people.

The story begins in the early years of this century, when the Russian scientist Ivan Petrovich Pavlov reported experiments in which he made dogs strongly fearful of a small chamber.[1] In the first stage of the experiment, while the animal was held in a harness in the chamber, a luminous circle was projected on a screen in front of it. That image was immediately followed by food. Soon the animal, on seeing the circle, would make food-approach responses: it would look at the food box, move forward to it, wag its tail, and salivate. When this behavior was well established, Pavlov began to intersperse projections of an elongated oval between projections of the circle. But the oval was never accompanied by feeding. The effect of this was that the oval, in contrast to the food-signaling circle, acquired the power to bring out "anti-feeding" responses, responses that actively inhibited feeding.

Pavlov demonstrated that this was happening in the following way. He counted the drops of saliva that the animal secreted when it saw the shapes singly or in combination. The circle alone would make the dog secrete, say, fifteen drops of saliva; the oval alone, zero. When the circle was accompanied by the oval, only seven drops would appear. The effect was not merely a matter of the animal's being distracted by the oval. This was shown by the fact that if some other shape, like a black square, accompanied the circle, there would be practically no diminution in the amount of saliva secreted. Here is a graphic presentation:

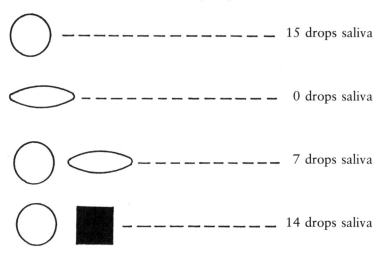

Clearly, the oval on the screen was actively inhibiting the animal's feeding responses.

Starting from these positive and negative conditionings, Pavlov now set about using this learning to create conflict in the animal. Instead of interspersing the original long oval between projections of the circle, he began to substitute an oval that was slightly less elongated. The animal would at first respond to this new and rounder oval by salivating slightly. But then, since this shape too was never followed by food, it came to have the same effect as the elongated oval; it actively countered the feeding response.

Pavlov then followed the same procedure with several progressively rounder ovals, each of which acquired "anti-feeding" power. Eventually the oval was so round that it was almost a circle. The dog, which up to that point had been able to distinguish between the circle and each successive oval, could no longer do so. It reacted both positively and negatively at the same time: the "round" oval aroused a strong impulse to eat (based on the circle) and a strong impulse not to eat (based on the ovals). The animal was, as Pavlov had intended, in a state of conflict. The conflict generated great anxiety. Pavlov wrote:

The whole behavior of the animal underwent an abrupt change. The hitherto quiet dog began to squeal in its stand, kept wriggling about . . . and bit through the tubes connecting the animal's room with the observer, a behavior which never happened before.[2]

The anxiety produced in this way became attached to the experimental chamber. Whenever the animal was brought into the experimental chamber, it barked violently and showed great distress. Furthermore, if the experimenter had been visible at the time of the conflict, fear would also have become conditioned to him. These conditioned fears were very persistent and would have remained with the animal for the rest of its life had it been left untreated. Pavlov applied the term *experimental neurosis* to the condition he had induced.

When I embarked on my own experimental work, I had the benefit of Pavlov's work as well as more than a dozen other studies on experimental neuroses that had been done in the United States.[3] Among these, a series of experiments by a Chicago psychiatrist, Dr. Jules Masserman,[4] were particularly important. He taught cats to feed in an experimental cage at the sound of a buzzer; each time a cat heard the sound, it would dart forward to raise the lid of the food box. Then one day Masserman shocked an animal just as it made the move forward. After a few shocks under these circumstances, the animal became continuously and lastingly fearful in the experimental cage. (Masserman believed that the anxiety came about because of conflict between the feeding response and the response to the shock.)

Masserman described the first successful behavioral treatment of experimental neurosis. Inside the cage was a movable partition. He put food in the food box and then used the partition to force the cat toward it. When the animal's nose was close to the food, it would usually eat, at first in hurried gulps, and then gradually more and more readily, while its fear would progressively diminish.

The first experiments I did repeated these procedures, with similar results. I then introduced a variation to see whether conflict between the feeding response and the response to shock really had the causal role that Masserman supposed. I simply shocked each of several animals in the experimental cage without ever having fed them there. Fear of the cage was induced in this way just as surely as when shock disrupted feeding. *Electric shock alone was thus clearly sufficient to produce the experimental neurosis.* (In Pavlov's experiment with circles and ovals, by contrast, conflict was the real and only source of fear.)

This was the key discovery, for it showed that the experimental neurosis was not produced by conflict exclusively. With this new information in hand, I turned my attention to treatment techniques. Since it was evident that the act of eating was somehow involved in weakening the anxiety, I decided to study the interrelations of eating and anxiety in a quantitative way.

I had induced neuroses in my cats by shocking them in a cage similar to that used by Masserman (40 by 20 by 20 inches), using (as he did) high-voltage, low-amperage current, which is painful but incapable of physically harming the animal. The experimental cage stood in a room containing a great deal of very dark wooden laboratory furniture. The animal, once it had been made neurotic, displayed fear anywhere in this room (though less than in the experimental cage itself). It was also fearful in other rooms, to a degree that always depended on the room's resemblance to the experimental room — an example of generalization. However, there was no fear in the living cages, which were very large (about 8 feet long, 5 feet wide, and 9 feet high) and were located on the roof of the medical school.

A striking feature of the neurosis was the animal's absolute refusal to eat in the experimental cage. Even if it had been deprived of food for twenty-four or forty-eight hours, it would refuse food dropped under its nose in that cage, though it might be left there with the food for days. Taking off from this observation, I reasoned as follows: If anxiety can inhibit a hungry animal from eating, that must mean that *the strength of the anxiety is greater than the eating drive of an animal that has starved for as long as forty-eight hours.* Therefore, if the relative strengths of the two arousals were reversed, that is, if the drive to eat was made the stronger, the animal would eat and *the fear would be inhibited.* In consequence, I hoped, the anxiety response habit would be weakened.

In order to try this out, I resorted to the various rooms mentioned above to which anxiety had generalized. Since anxiety was weakest in rooms that looked least like the experimental room, I started with these. One of them was a spacious, bright room with whitewashed walls and large windows — very different from the experimental room with its dark heavy furniture. A hungry animal was offered food in that room. It ate with hesitation at first, but then more and more readily, until, after perhaps twenty pellets of meat, it was actively searching for food. On the following experimental day, it would eat in the room next in order of resemblance to the experimental room, where it had previously refused to eat. Here, too, successive pellets of meat would be consumed more and more readily. Eventually, it would eat on the floor of the experimental room, and then in the experimental cage. It took patience and a large amount of food to remove entirely the anxiety that the experimental cage aroused — usually about two hundred pellets of meat over several days.

What these experiments showed was that *it is possible to overcome a fear habit by making an animal a little afraid at a time and combating the fear by feeding.* By keeping the amount of new fear small from one step to the next (from one room to the next), a very fearful situation was eventually completely defused. What was clearly involved here was mutual inhibition. When anxiety was the stronger impulse, eating was inhibited; when eating was the stronger, anxiety was inhibited.

It was during the preceding few years that I had been unsuccessfully using narcoanalysis to treat soldiers with war neuroses. While the animal experiments were being carried out, the human cases were never out of mind. But I did not know how the reciprocal (mutual) inhibition principle could be applied to them. Since I was aware that children's fears had also been successfully treated by counterposed feeding, it was natural to try this out on the fears of human adults. The attempts failed dismally. For reasons that are unknown, and by a process that remains to be unraveled, in the course of human maturation feeding loses the emotional power that in children enables it to compete with anxiety.

The first responses I used successfully to compete with the anxiety of adults were the expression of anger and resentment. About a year later, I discovered the technique of active realization devised by Edmund Jacobson,[5] and I realized that the calmness that it produced might be used to counter anxiety. At first I followed Jacobson in trying to train people to relax so well that they could overcome the anxiety whenever it occurred in the course of their lives. But in most people this was extremely difficult to achieve, because the strength of anxiety in these situations could not be controlled. So I tried presenting weak disturbing scenes to the *imagination* of the deeply relaxed patient. With the first few individuals, I presented only one scene per session, because of certain cautionary statements by Pavlov. I believed that if the patient was still fearful from a scene when I asked him to imagine it a second time, the "leftover" fear would combine with fear from the second presentation to *raise* the total level, thus defeating the purpose of the relaxation.

One day things changed. While desensitizing a patient, I noticed that the more fear he felt from imagining a scene, the more he would move his right index finger away from the middle finger. So, having had him imagine a scene and noting the movements in his hand, with great trepidation I had him imagine the scene again. The index finger moved less! This was a thrilling experience and the real origin of desensitization—for it meant that one could with advantage present a scene more than once at a session. If a scene evoking weak anxiety was presented repeatedly, the successive repetitions produced less and less anxiety, and, finally, none at all.

V

Systematic Desensitization

Most of the behavior therapy techniques for treating useless fears parallel the treatment of experimental neurosis described in the previous chapter. This is very clear in the commonest technique, systematic desensitization; but a method was described long before the experiments were done that is even more similar to them.

An Early Method

Until about a half-century ago, there were no scientifically established guidelines for treating useless fears. Then, about 1920, the originator of the behaviorist movement, Dr. John B. Watson, was prompted by earlier experiments on learning to suggest certain procedures that could reasonably be tried.[1] One of these was the introduction, in the presence of the fear response, of other responses that might compete with fear. A few years later, Dr. Mary Cover Jones, a psychologist at the University of California at Berkeley who had been a student of Watson's, applied this suggestion to the treatment of children's fears, and was impressively successful in a number of cases. In a now classic paper published in 1924, she described the treatment of a 3-year-old boy named Peter, who had a great fear of rabbits and lesser fears of fur coats, feathers, and cotton.[2]

The child was placed in a high chair at one end of a long room and given candy of his choice. While he was eating, a young woman brought a rabbit in through a door at the other end of the room and gradually advanced as Peter watched, until he stopped eating. She then moved back slowly until the rabbit was at a sufficient distance no longer to interfere with the child's eating. After a while, the rabbit could be brought a little closer without causing Peter to stop eating. With frequent treatment sessions over a period of two months, it became possible for Peter to go on eating with the rabbit progressively closer. Eventually he could hold the rabbit on his lap without showing any fear. Dr. Jones noted that the fears of the cotton, the fur coat, and the feathers had also been weakened. When presented with these objects, Peter looked at them, handled them, and then turned to something that interested him more. These objects had possessed fear-arousing power only to the extent that they shared the furriness of the rabbit—an instance of generalization.

At her last session with Peter, Dr. Jones wanted to see what he would do if confronted by a *different* animal. The question was whether the fear might also have been attached to animal features not found in rabbits. Accordingly, she placed in front of Peter a mouse and a tangled mass of angleworms. At first he was slightly uneasy and moved away, but in a few minutes he was carrying the worms and watching the mouse with undisturbed interest. Thus, it was the furriness alone that had been frightening, and no other feature of animals.

Clearly, Dr. Jones's use of feeding hardly differs at all from the treatment of the experimental neuroses described in Chapter IV. It has again in recent years been used to treat children's fears, but, as mentioned earlier, it is ineffective in adults.

Although her work was published in 1924, it aroused very little interest at the time. (Dr. Jones told me, when I first met her at Berkeley in 1956, that she had received only three requests for reprints and had been so disheartened that she turned to other areas of research.) I learned of her work during the course of my experiments and was encouraged by it, as it indicated that my treatment of animal neuroses was applicable to human beings.

The Technique of Systematic Desensitization

Systematic desensitization is the most commonly used method of behavior therapy. *Desensitization* refers to what is brought about in the patient: he becomes less and less sensitive to whatever has been triggering his fear. *Systematic* means that the therapist follows a rule: only after he has accomplished the desensitization at one level of fear does he proceed to the next level. He is thus using a system that dictates the sequence of events in therapy.

The technique is directly modeled on the feeding method that solved the problem of the experimental neuroses. It consists of exposing the patient, while he was in a state of emotional calmness, to a small "dose" of something he fears. The calmness, which is used in place of feeding to compete with fear, is usually attained through deep relaxation of the patient's muscles, and the fearful object is presented not in reality but *in the patient's imagination*. This not only allows the therapist to present a virtually limitless range of objects and situations; it enables him to control precisely the beginning and ending of each presentation.

The essence of the procedure is to have the calmed patient visualize a slightly fearful image for a few seconds at a time. With each repetition, the amount of fear lessens, soon going down to zero. Then successively more fearful images are treated in the same way, until even the most fearful eventually loses its fear-arousing power. The following is a detailed account, first of the preliminaries to systematic desensitization, and then of the procedure itself.

Measuring Fear

Ordinary language is not very successful in communicating how much fear a person is experiencing. In response to the question "How afraid do you feel right now?" several people might reply, "Quite a bit"; but measurements of their pulse rate, blood pressure, and skin responses by a polygraph would probably show large differences of arousal from person to person. Since not every therapist has a polygraph handy, and since it is cumbersome to use anyway, it is a great advantage to have a way of quantifying people's *feelings* of fear. A standard practice in behavior therapy is to set up what is called a *subjective anxiety scale*.

The idea of such a scale is introduced to the patient in the following words: "Think of the worst anxiety you have ever had or can imagine having and call it one hundred—that is maximum fear. Then think of being absolutely calm and call that zero. At every waking moment your fear level must be somewhere between zero and one hundred. Where is it right now?" Whatever the answer, whether it is zero, 35, or 80, the statement continues, "You will also be able to use the scale to tell me by how much you would expect your fear level to be raised by particular situations among those that you fear." With some practice, most people are able to evaluate with assurance the strength of their fears. Later on, the scale is used to enable a person to report the strength of his reactions to scenes presented during desensitization.

Here are some descriptions of anxiety that an individual may learn to equate with the various levels on the scale:

0	No anxiety at all; complete calmness.
1–10	Very slight anxiety.
10–20	Slight anxiety.
20–40	Moderate anxiety; definitely unpleasant feeling.
40–60	Severe anxiety; considerable distress.
60–80	Severe anxiety; becoming intolerable.
80–100	Very severe anxiety; approaching panic.

Pinpointing the Fear Sources

How does the therapist identify the fears that will figure in the hierarchy? He begins by examining the presenting complaint. If, for instance, it is discomfort at being in a crowd, the heart of the fear may simply be a matter of the number of people present. In other cases, it may be the fact that the patient is the focus of people's attention (even if he is not doing anything), or the fact that he is seen to perform in some formal way (like giving a presentation). In still other cases, he needs only to be seen engaging in casual conversation in order to experience anxiety.

However, it may become apparent that these more concrete aspects of the presenting complaints show themselves inadequate to explain the anxiety. The therapist then moves on to more extensive probing and questioning of the patient. In the beginning, this process may be little more than educated guesswork. Some starting points will immediately suggest themselves—having to do with time and place, and the details of circumstances according to which the levels of anxiety may change. The therapist behaves something like a bee buzzing around a flower, hovering and changing directions, landing in several places before alighting at just the right spot. And more often than not this leads to other direct hits, as the fear complex is given shape and definition bit by bit. Certain lines of questioning may lead nowhere. But armed with a knowledge of the *kinds* of things he is looking for, the therapist develops a sense of where he may begin to see a dimension emerge. There is a very definite collaborative aspect to this search-and-name game; the therapist cannot do it without the patient—based on some theoretical idea of what he is *supposed* to find. As a certain line starts to show some promise, the questioning becomes more focused and precise.

An example of this less obvious probing is the following: A 28-year-old nurse named Fay complained of being nervous at work and in social situations. Though she was very attractive, she had been shying away from men and had never really had a satisfying relationship. Fay expressed the presenting complaint at that time in this way: "I feel ill-at-ease around people. I'm uncomfortable at work, or even just walking on the street. I have a high anxiety level a lot of the time." The problem underlying all her difficulties turned out to be anxiety about what other people might be thinking of her. If she were at a party, for instance, she would imagine that they were thinking, "She dresses in bad taste." While at work, Fay would often worry that the supervisor was thinking that she had not been conscientious or diligent enough. She had recently begun taking piano lessons. Any remark from her teacher that could possibly be construed as negative would devastate her; she would say to herself, "He doesn't really think I have any talent or that I'm worth his time to teach." All these fears came from thoughts about herself that Fay projected into the minds of others. That this was the case could only be learned from suggesting hypotheses and exploring their appropriateness with her. The hierarchy consisted of these projected thoughts and not of the external situations that were the setting for her anxieties.

The anxiety elicited by the projected thoughts was a joint function of the content of the thoughts and of the person into whose mind she projected them. There was, therefore, a two-dimensional hierarchy which is shown later in this chapter. In the actual desensitization, she would imagine overhearing a statement being made about her by a particular person, going in ascending order of the numerical values shown in the hierarchy.

Ranking the Fear Sources: The Hierarchy

The therapist explores with the patient a wide range of familiar situations that are fearful, and has the patient list them. Since there may be several categories of fear-provoking situations, there may be several lists. A particular person may have, say, three lists—of strange places, failures, and heights. Then, working together, he and the therapist rearrange the items in each list in order of the amount of fear elicited by the situations. The ranked list is called a *hierarchy*. Take the simple example of the fear of heights: he may be slightly anxious when looking out of a second-floor window, and more and more anxious as he goes higher. The listed heights, differing by approximately equal increases in fear arousal, make up a height hierarchy. The numerical sequence of heights that will increase fear in equal steps varies from case to case. A typical sequence would be second floor, third, fifth, seventh, tenth, thirteenth, sixteenth, twentieth, twenty-fifth, thirtieth, fortieth. At the greater heights, it takes more elevation to increase fear a given amount.

The lists relating to fears of heights are usually simple in that they increase in a single "dimension," namely height. The same is true of many other phobias, such as those of enclosed spaces (claustrophobia), darkness, and harmless animals. The fear of a spider, for example, may increase solely with the proximity of the animal, and of darkness solely with the degree of darkness.

But fears often vary in more than one dimension, even in "simple" phobias. A fear of spiders may vary not only with proximity, but also with other dimensions: the size of the animal, its color, the character of its movements, whether or not it is caged, whether it is alive or dead, etc. In the case of the young woman with social fears described above, the amount of fear depended on two interacting factors — the presumed negative evaluation, for example, "selfish," "poor dress sense," and the person to whom the opinion was attributed. This is an example of a two-dimensional hierarchy.

In certain cases, the fear sources are so outwardly different that they cannot be neatly contained in a single dimension, like size or height or number. The hierarchy is then determined not by some external physical measure, but by the particular feeling that the situations arouse in the individual. For instance, there is little physical similarity between a tight ring on the finger and an elevator, but when each causes the same feeling of confinement in a person, they are grouped in the same hierarchy. This feeling of confinement is what creates the anxiety; the situations are then ranked according to how much anxiety they arouse.

Four examples of such hierarchies are given below. The figures to the right indicate the anxiety levels for the respective items. Notice that the items are in *descending* order, which means that treatment will start at the *bottom* of each list.

Hierarchy Items	Anxiety Level
Fear of Being Belittled	
1. Derisive remarks made by husband.	85
2. Derisive remarks made by friends.	75
3. Sarcasm from husband or friends.	70
4. Being nagged about shortcomings.	60
5. Remarks in a conversation being ignored.	40–50
6. Not being invited to the party of an office associate.	35
7. Being excluded from a group activity.	25
8. Not being invited to the party of an acquaintance.	15
9. Awareness of a patronizing attitude from anybody.	5
Death-Related Fears	
1. Seeing a dead man in a coffin.	100
2. Being at a burial.	90
3. Seeing a burial assemblage from a distance.	80
4. Reading the obituary notice of a young person who dies of a heart attack.	70

5. Driving past a cemetery
   (the nearer, the worse).   55–65
6. Seeing a funeral (the nearer, the worse).   40–55
7. Passing a funeral home
   (the nearer, the worse).   30–40
8. Reading the obituary notice of an old person.   25
9. Being inside a hospital.   20
10. Seeing a hospital.   10
11. Seeing an ambulance.   5

Fear of Own Symptoms (Despite Knowing Them to be Insignificant)

1. Fluttering heart.   90
2. Shooting pains in chest and abdomen.   80
3. Pains in left shoulder and back.   70
4. Pain on top of head.   55
5. Buzzing in ears.   45
6. Trembling of hands.   35
7. Numbness or pain in fingertips.   25
8. Shortness of breath after exertion.   20
9. Pain in left hand (from an old injury).   10

Fear of What People Think (A Bi-dimensional Hierarchy—Fay)

	George	Dad	Andrea	Freda	Doorman
Selfish	75	60	50	40	25
Not good looking	60	45	40	30	20
Poor dress taste	55	35	35	25	20
Aloof	45	30	25	20	10
Not industrious	40	25	20	15	0

The practical reason for hierarchies is that they enable the therapist to deal with fear in small amounts at a time. It is important to have relatively uniform differences between adjacent items of a hierarchy. Usually the difference is about 10 units. This is somewhat like designing a staircase: the stairs must be climbable. If there is too great a gap between any two steps, it becomes difficult or impossible for one to ascend them. On the other hand, if the steps are too low, there are too many of them and too much horizontal distance is needed to ascend to a given height. However, while it is generally practical to have about ten steps in a hierarchy, some require many more.

Deep Muscle Relaxation

As in the treatment of animal neuroses, the weakening of human fear habits requires the action of another response that can compete with fear. Whereas in the cats the competing response was feeding, in systematic desensitization it is calmness, which, as mentioned before, is typically procured by deep muscle relaxation.

Deep muscle relaxation has physiological and emotional effects that are the opposite of those of anxiety. The pulse rate slows, the blood pressure decreases, the breathing becomes slower and more even, digestive activity is enhanced, and sweating of the palms is diminished. Calmness accompanies these effects; if it is opposed to a low level of anxiety, it will counteract (inhibit) the anxiety.

Relaxation training begins with the muscles of the arms, because these lend themselves readily to the experience of muscle tension. The therapist holds the patient's right wrist and asks her to bend her elbow against resistance, thus strongly contracting her biceps. He then instructs the patient to let go gradually, until her forearm comes to rest again in its original horizontal position on the arm of the armchair. While the forearm is descending, the patient's attention is drawn to the fact that a progressive undoing of tension is taking place in the biceps. When the forearm has come to rest on the armchair, the patient is asked, nevertheless, to continue the untensing — to try to go farther and farther in the negative direction. She must continue untensing the biceps for about ten minutes, during which time she must report any unusual sensations, such as warmth or tingling of the fingers, heaviness or lightness of the limbs, changes in depth of breathing, and any emotional changes. She is told that her ability to relax and to calm herself will increase with practice, to which she should apply at least two concentrated periods of fifteen minutes each day. In addition, it is a good idea to relax muscles for short periods when they are not in use. For example, the arm muscles can be relaxed while she is having a conversation, since there is then no particular use for them under most circumstances.

The number of muscle groups to be trained in relaxation at a session varies. As a general rule, all the muscles of the arms and forearms will be taught at the first session, the muscles of the forehead and those controlling the movements of the lips at the second, the jaws and tongue at the third, the neck and shoulders at the fourth, the muscles of the trunk at the fifth, and the legs and thighs at the sixth. In general, ten to fifteen minutes of a session are devoted to relaxation training, while the rest of the time is spent on such other activities as the discussion of recent experiences, assertiveness training, and hierarchy construction. It is crucial to realize that the aim of relaxation training is not muscle control per se, but emotional calmness. Many people are able to achieve this well enough within three or four sessions, so that for the purposes of desensitization it often turns out that training need not extend beyond the top half of the body.

Deep relaxation is different from what we ordinarily refer to as "relaxing." Reading a good book, going fishing, lying around in the sun on a summer's day, puttering about in the garden are relaxing activities. But *active* relaxation is what is required for the purposes of desensitization. This means a relaxation that is more profound, and more focused on our muscles, than accompanies the above recreational activities. The person is taught to locate, one by one, the muscles in his various body zones: his face, forehead, jaws, tongue, eyes, neck, shoulders, arms, back, abdomen, thighs, lower legs, and feet. Once he has located a muscle, he is taught to relax it. He establishes where a muscle is by tightening it according to instructions. Then he is shown how to let go, and to keep on letting go beyond the point that he would normally think of as "relaxed." It is through *actively relaxing* muscles past their normal resting state that most of the anti-anxiety physiological effects take place. The pulse slows down, the palms dry up, and so on. As with any other skill, relaxing becomes easier with practice. The individual learns to detect the feelings that indicate relaxation in his body, such as warmth or heaviness, or tingling sensations. These feelings differ from person to person, and some people have none at all.

People who have exceptional control of their muscles, like athletes and dancers, are particularly good relaxers. But it is not necessary that one be a dancer or an athlete for this technique to work; a person is *taught* to relax, and through practice increases his or her skill.

Desensitization Procedure

When the hierarchies have been put together and the patient is able adequately to calm himself, we are ready to begin systematic desensitization. The patient, sitting or lying in a comfortable position, is asked to close his eyes. The therapist then tells him to relax in the way that he has practiced, and follows this general instruction by directing attention to each group of muscles in turn, usually proceeding downward from the head region to the legs.

After a few minutes, the therapist ascertains the patient's anxiety level. If it is zero, he asks the patient to imagine for a few seconds the "weakest"—the least disturbing—scene from a hierarchy. As a rule, while the scene lasts, it breaks into the calmness and arouses a small amount of anxiety. The patient is asked to stop imagining the scene and to try to return to the original level of calmness by resuming concentration on relaxing the muscles. This usually takes fifteen to thirty seconds, and the patient indicates it by a prearranged word such as "okay." With subsequent presentations, the anxiety decreases, so that after several presentations (usually three or four), the scene elicits no anxiety at all. Then the next scene in the hierarchy is introduced. In the course of a varying number of sessions, the "strongest" scene in the hierarchy will totally lose its ability to evoke anxiety. *In general, there is a close relationship between the reduction of a person's anxiety responses to imagined situations and to the corresponding real situations.*

For illustration, let us refer to the hierarchy of death-related fears listed earlier in this chapter. The lowest item, seeing an ambulance, had been given in advance a rating of 5 units of anxiety. When the patient *imagined* seeing an ambulance while in a state of deep muscle relaxation, the 5 units due to that image were partially inhibited, so that he felt only 2 units. And when he imagined that scene again a minute later, while still deeply relaxed, the anxiety decreased to zero. That scene was no longer fearful.

Now an interesting and characteristic thing happened. When the anxiety from the weakest scene (the ambulance) had been brought down to zero, the second weakest scene (the hospital) evoked 5 units instead of its original 10. So its anxiety was now small enough to be further diminished by the opposing calmness. In this way, step by step, it was possible to advance up the scale until finally the most powerful situation, seeing a dead man in a coffin, only evoked 5 or 10 units of anxiety. This, too, could then be overcome, so that the entire fear system was eliminated.

The procedure, to be effective, must produce and bring together at the right time the events that are necessary to bring about change. The relaxation must actually lower anxiety to zero. Then, the imagining must be realistic in the sense that the patient *actually responds with anxiety* to what he imagines. Most people can imagine clearly and respond emotionally to the images much as they would to the real situation.[3] When the real event evokes anxiety, then conjuring it up in imagination usually does so as well. (Even in the therapist's office, some people tremble and feel anxious when recounting events that have upset them.)

In the minority whose imagined scenes evoke little or no anxiety, it may be possible to enhance the emotional reaction by adding details to the scene, or by having the individual describe the scene as he is creating it instead of receiving it passively. If these efforts fail, the therapist will have to make use of real situations or pictures. For example, for one who fears spiders, a real spider in a glass container may be brought into the office; in a fear of heights, one may resort to systematic exposure to increasing heights.

The Technique in an Actual Case

Let us look at an instance of systematic desensitization in the treatment of a very common problem. Leonard, aged 31, a sales representative, had an oversensitivity to rejection. The items of his hierarchy were, as usual, written in *descending* order of their anxiety-producing effects. The anxiety values are noted in the right column.

Hierarchy Items	Anxiety Value
1. His apology for a blunder is not accepted by a friend.	80
2. His invitation to a friend to his apartment for dinner or drinks is refused.	70
3. He speaks to a colleague who does not seem to hear.	60
4. A project important to him is criticized by colleagues.	50
5. He is left out of social plans or not invited.	40
6. He is spoken to by a colleague in a voice stronger than the speaker uses to others present.	25
7. Nobody remembers his birthday.	25
8. His greeting to an acquaintance he passes in the street is not returned.	15

Having constructed this hierarchy with Leonard, I said to him: "Your eyes being closed, I am going to ask you to imagine a number of scenes. You will imagine them very clearly. The moment the image I suggest is clearly formed, indicate it by raising your left index finger about an inch."

In the hierarchy given above, I started, of course, with the weakest item, number 8, in the following words: "Walking in the street on a pleasant Monday morning, you see yourself approaching a man to whom you spoke for ten minutes at a party the previous Saturday night. You smile in greeting, but he walks past with a blank stare." When Leonard's finger rose to indicate that he had the scene, I let about five seconds pass, stopped the scene, and then asked by how much the anxiety level rose during the visualization. He said, "Fifteen units." When the scene was presented a second time after a period of relaxation, the anxiety rose only 8 units; the third time it was 3 units; and the fourth time zero. Then I began presentations of the next scene on the hierarchy—number 7—in this way: "It is five P.M. on your birthday; neither your wife nor your close friends have remembered." This was presented repeatedly in the same way as the first scene. I mentioned a specific time (5:00 P.M.) for this item because anxiety increased with increasing lateness. (It also increased with larger numbers of unremembering friends.) Eventually, Leonard was able to imagine without any anxiety even the strongest item in the hierarchy.

But the change was not confined to what was imagined. It *transferred* to the corresponding real situations. This is in keeping with psychological studies which have found that an individual's responses are similar to real and imagined sights, to real and imagined sounds, and so on.[4] It also extended beyond the specific social interactions that were dealt with in the treatment to a whole array of similar situations, because of generalization. If the hierarchy has been skillfully put together and has covered the ground adequately, the patient will no longer be unnecessarily disturbed by any rejections.

Illustrations of Systematic Desensitization

FRANK, a 23-year-old street-car driver, entered the consulting room in a state of high anxiety. Eight hours earlier a woman had walked in front of his slowly moving trolley. She had been "knocked out and her head was bleeding." Although a doctor said that the woman's injury was not serious, Frank had become increasingly shaky and had developed severe abdominal pain. He had gotten over previous accidents in an hour or two, but in these no human injury had been involved.

The significance of human injury lay in the fact that when Frank was 13, his father had died in a bloody accident, and ever since he had had a fear of human blood. Even the tiny bead of blood that might appear on his face during shaving gave him an uncomfortable feeling. He was quite unaffected by animal blood; he had seen live-stock killed and had himself cut the throats of fowl. It seemed certain that his grossly excessive reaction to the accident was due to his phobia of *human* blood.

The first five interviews, which took place over six days, were confined to obtaining a picture of Frank's personality and background and to having him overcome his immediate disturbed state by learning and practicing relaxation. At the fifth interview he reported feeling very well. I told him to drive a street car again for a short distance, which he did later that day, without any ill effect.

At the sixth interview, we ranked various situations involving human blood, in order of their disturbing effect. At this and later interviews, Frank was relaxed and was asked to visualize "blood situations." The feeblest scene was a slightly blood-tinged bandage lying in a basket. When this no longer disturbed his relaxation, I asked him to imagine a tiny drop of blood on his own face while shaving, and had him evoke this image several times, until anxiety ceased. With the "conquest" of two or three images at each session, it was possible for Frank eventually to reach the stage at which he could visualize a casualty ward full of injured people and not be made anxious by the mental picture.

The relation of change during treatment to change in real life was revealed in Frank's case in a most dramatic way. Two days before his last interview, he saw a man knocked over by a motorcycle. The victim was seriously injured and bleeding profusely. Frank was unperturbed by the blood, and when the ambulance arrived, he helped to load the victim into it.

FLORENCE, a 24-year-old woman, had experienced repeated failures because of the great anxiety she felt during university examinations. We established the following hierarchy (in *descending* order of anxiety):

Hierarchy Items	Anxiety Values
1. On the way to the university on the day of an examination.	95
2. In the process of answering an examination paper.	90
3. Standing before the unopened doors of the examination room.	80
4. Awaiting the distribution of examination papers.	70
5. When the examination papers are lying face down before her.	60
6. The night before an examination.	50
7. One day before an examination.	40
8. Two days before an examination.	30
9. Three days before an examination.	20
10. Four days before an examination.	15
11. A week before an examination.	10

The reader should note that in the top five items the strength of the fear was not strictly related to the proximity of the examination; but such "illogical" variations are common, for *the emotional part of the nervous system obeys the laws of conditioning, not the rules of logic.* Freedom from anxiety to the highest items of this hierarchy was achieved in seven sessions of desensitization. Four months later, this young woman took (and passed) her university examinations without any anxiety.

STUART, 31, was an advertising salesman who was afraid of being with people, especially when he found it difficult to get away. This fear made him want to urinate. In recent months, if he had to spend just five minutes in the office of a client, he became anxious and had a strong desire to urinate. If he went out and relieved himself, the urge would come back after another five minutes. He was also anxious in such public places as trains and airplanes, shopping centers, and anywhere that a crowd had gathered.

After careful questioning, it became clear that Stuart's fear worked in the following way. His need to urinate was triggered by a certain level of anxiety. Once he entered a client's office, his anxiety gradually built over the course of five minutes until it reached that critical level. Then, as he felt the need to urinate, a new source of fear entered the picture: that he might wet his pants in front of the client. The two combined fears made his anxiety level shoot up close to panic. The treatment strategy, therefore, would be to defuse the fear he felt *before* the added fear of wetting his pants was set off. To desensitize him, I had to make certain that the first imagined scenes would be structured in such a way that he spent much less than the critical five minutes with his client.

Stuart's case illustrates the flexibility that is gained through the use of the imagination. He was asked to imagine that he was interviewing a client who had a strict rule: the client would see no sales representative for more than two minutes. This meant that Stuart's anxiety level would be at a manageable level, one that could be overcome by active relaxation. The length of time was then gradually increased, until he could comfortably imagine himself spending several hours in a client's office. His fear of urinating correspondingly receded and disappeared. Another consequence of the diminishing fear of being with people was that he lost his fear of planes, trains, crowds, and so forth.

But Stuart had another, unrelated problem: jealousy. He had never gotten over the fact that when he met the woman who was to become his wife, she told him that she had had a previous affair. He was 18 at the time, and, indeed, he broke off the relationship when he learned this. He then reconsidered and decided that he could live with it, and at the age of 20 he married her, even though he felt that he had a "soiled bill of goods," to use his expression. Nevertheless, he continued to be obsessed with the thought of his wife consorting with the other man.

Jealousy is often based on anxiety, and I treated him in the following way. I had him imagine that someone had taken movies of his wife's behavior with her lover. In this way, Stuart could picture his wife and the man as they were then — as he pictured them in his obsession — but in segments that I could control by determining the precise content of each film. In the first one, the other man was holding his wife's hand. I repeated that scene until Stuart had no more anxiety. The second movie (that he imagined) had his wife sitting on a couch with her lover, who kissed her and then put his hand on her breast over her dress for exactly eight seconds. Stuart felt a fair amount of anxiety, which was overcome in three presentations. Gradually, the length of time during which the hand was on the breast was increased, from one film to the next, to three minutes, with the wife snuggling up to her lover. We were prepared to go further with the scenes, but there was no need. When Stuart lost his anxiety about that last scene, he said that once she could be caressed for three minutes and encourage her lover by snuggling up to him, there was a *commitment* on her part. If that didn't bother him, nothing would. And that was the end of his jealous obsession.

Stuart's case also shows an interesting feature of some fear complexes. One minute had been worse than thirty seconds, and two minutes worse than one minute. But once three minutes and the idea of commitment were reached, there was no need for the imagined scenes to go on longer or show heavier petting. Stuart's "boiling point," so to speak, had been reached, and turning up the flame any higher would not have made the water hotter. It oftens happens that after fear of a situation that is ranked at, say, 80 on the hierarchy has been overcome, there is no need to continue to 90 and then 100. The core of the fear has been effectively removed.

Variations of Desensitization

There are cases in which desensitization using imagery does not succeed, and there are different reasons for this. Some people do not respond fearfully when they *imagine* the things they find fearful in the real world. With them, it is necessary for the therapist to present the real objects—either concretely or in photographs—while the patient is in a state of relaxation. With fears of easily accessible objects—of insects, say, or animals such as dogs—a method that is often very effective is *modeling*. The patient watches a fearless model (who may be the therapist or some other person) making progressively closer approaches to the feared object, and later, with the guidance of the model, makes gradual approaches himself.

Desensitization also fails with patients who cannot relax or in whom relaxation does not produce emotional calming. Sometimes the effects of relaxation can be increased by hypnosis. There are also people who are unable to relax because of a conditioned fear of "letting go." For them, there are several other ways of inhibiting anxiety.[5] One way is to employ imagination to arouse other emotions—pleasurable emotions—by sexual scenes, images of skiing, or floating on the waves, or whatever else "turns on" the individual. Another involves progressive exposure of the patient to feared situations when he has been calmed by a tranquilizing drug, a method that can be used only by a physician and demands careful monitoring.

Some people experience a state of continuous anxiety known as "free-floating" anxiety, which prevents them from being sufficiently calm for desensitization to be effective. This kind of anxiety is triggered by ever-present conditions, such as the sensation of one's own body, light or darkness, the passage of time, or city noises. The person who suffers from this form of anxiety never has it in isolation; he is *also* sensitive to specific fears, whether or not he knows it. We may take the example of a man who, after a traumatic sexual experience, developed sexual fears based on anxiety. During that traumatic experience, since the bedroom light was off, he could see only the dark outlines of objects. As a result, anxiety was attached also to dark outlines, wherever he might encounter them; of course, they are common in everyday life.

Free-floating anxiety can be temporarily erased in a most dramatic way by the person's taking a few intermittent inhalations of a mixture of carbon dioxide and oxygen.[6] This lowers the anxiety level to such an extent that desensitization can be successfully carried out, and the decrement usually lasts for several hours. It may sometimes last for weeks. This happened in the case just described. During this time, the man was not disturbed by the dark outlines of objects. But if in those weeks he had had a sexual experience that raised his anxiety level, *the free-floating anxiety response to dark outlines would have been brought back;* the anxiety would have become reconditioned to the dark outlines of objects. The only way it could be permanently removed was for the therapist to eliminate the specific sexual anxiety, using desensitization.

Do It Yourself: How Much Can You Do?

The idea behind systematic desensitization is really quite simple: break a big problem down into smaller, manageable ones. If it is so simple, then why can't people do it themselves at home? Unfortunately, most of the time this is not possible, for various reasons. The "right" scenes are not always easy to identify. The behavior analysis is often difficult to make correctly. If the analysis is incorrect, it will not be possible to advance up the hierarchy, or an impasse will be reached after the first new steps. In addition, for relaxation to produce calmness, it must be correctly taught and practiced. And, as we have seen, the different scenes must be selected and ranked appropriately, a task that usually requires the close collaboration of the therapist and the patient.

There are other problems. The scene must be imagined *identically* each time it is presented. The amount of time a scene is presented must be carefully controlled, a very difficult task to undertake by oneself. Some people are unable to keep to the scene; their minds wander. Often, a patient indicates that he is responding fearfully to a scene, but he is really saying what he *would* feel if the situation were actually happening. He is not, in fact, experiencing the emotion *now*. In neither of these circumstances will therapeutic change occur. Then, too, the relaxation must be *emotionally* effective: some people can relax their muscles without producing any anxiety-countering emotion, and desensitization will not work. When a person seems not to be calmed when he relaxes, a therapist may use a polygraph to see what is really happening.

It is, nevertheless, interesting to note that people sometimes use a kind of desensitization to overcome their own anxieties without any awareness of the technicalities. I once met a man who had been a navigator on a B-52 during World War II and had been forced to parachute from the plane when it was shot down. As a result of that experience, he had developed a fear of heights and of flying, and had been transferred to a cartography unit. His new duties included looking at relief maps through stereoscopic glasses that made the terrain on the maps seem to be viewed from a very great height. As he was repeatedly exposed to this sight in a "safe" situation—sitting at a desk in an office—he gradually lost his fear and was once again able to resume flying. He had inadvertently desensitized himself. Similarly, a mother whose baby is terrified by the advancing waves on a beach holds him at the water's edge and dips his feet in the waves by degrees. She is desensitizing him to the ocean, and soon he is having fun and smiling at the deeper immersions.

I have pointed out some of the many drawbacks and pitfalls of attempting systematic self-desensitization, but I should add that a person who attempts it can hardly do himself harm and may very well do some good. There are many people who, through yoga, meditation, dance, or other activities, have learned to calm themselves; others have learned deep muscle relaxation by following the instructions in a book of Edmund Jacobson's entitled *You Must Relax*.[7] Since there are not, unfortunately, enough behavior therapists to go around, these people may profitably attempt to do by themselves what would better be done in conjunction with a therapist. This may include trying to switch on their practiced state of calm in a variety of life situations. They should keep in mind, though, that a failure to make progress may be due to any one of, or a combination of, the abovementioned difficulties.

Certain stress management programs that concentrate on teaching deep muscle relaxation may be of tremendous value to people who are unable to find a qualified behavior therapist.[8]

important than one's own. Often that teaching has a religious basis, but it may also derive from the "high standards of conduct" demanded by parents. I once treated a 36-year-old man whose parents had strongly insisted on polite submissiveness. During World War II, at the age of 8, he had gone to live for two years with an uncle and aunt who encouraged self-expression. He thrived in this environment and became a much more attractive personality. Unfortunately, his new behavior was severely punished by his parents when he returned home. The result was a pervasive fear of self-expression, especially toward authority figures, that had persisted all these years.

The nature of interpersonal fearfulness varies widely. Some people are unassertive with almost everybody. In others, the problem exists only in particular contexts. They can competently conduct their affairs with shopkeepers and strangers, but are timorous and submissive toward anyone important, like a mother, a wife, a boss, or a lover—or toward only some of these. By contrast, there are those who dominate (and occasionally tyrannize over) close associates, but are fearful, awkward, and in various degrees ineffective in their dealings with outsiders.

Before assertiveness training can begin, a person must recognize that it is reasonable. He will obviously not be receptive if he believes that it is morally good always to place the interests of others ahead of his own. It is true that there are certain people, saints and martyrs among them, who adopt self-sacrifice as a guiding principle—but they do it from strength. This is in stark contrast to the individual who always puts others ahead of himself because he is pussyfooting through life at the mercy of his useless fears. Some of the most severe cases are those people who have been taught to turn the other cheek. They must be made to understand that this is not a useful rule for ordinary mortals. They are shown the practicality and morality of the rule of thumbs that, in many areas of life, a person must consider himself first and *then* take into account the interests of others. This morality is expressed in the famous statement of Hillel, most renowned of the ancient Talmudic Fathers: "If I am not for myself, who will be for me? And if I am for myself only, what am I?"

Most people are easily convinced of the need for appropriate assertiveness. Some have always been aware of it. In any event, awareness is not enough. They must learn how to take action. Simple direct coaxing is often all that one needs. If one sees the disadvantages of nonassertion—its frequently unpleasant emotional consequences and the unfavorable image it gives to others—assertive acts become easier and anxiety lessens. The power to assert grows like a snowball rolling down a slope.

Teaching Assertiveness

In assertiveness training, the therapist is in a sense killing two birds with one stone: he mobilizes emotions such as anger which compete with and inhibit the anxiety, and he teaches the patient appropriate modes of verbal and motor expression.

The therapist asks certain standard questions, such as:

- What do you do when someone gets in front of you in line?
- What do you do when the cashier in a department store rings up someone else's purchase before yours, even though you were clearly there first and had been waiting?
- What do you do if you are walking out of a shop and you notice that you have been short-changed by five dollars?

If the patient has behaved unassertively in any or all of these situations, they are used as starting points for changes in behavior. For example, he is instructed to say politely to the intruder in the line, "Excuse me—this is a line. Would you mind getting to the back of it?" Even if the standard situations are not directly relevant to the patient, they will suggest others that are, and these can then be used as the basis for instructions for future occasions. The patient is asked to be on the lookout for occurrences that lend themselves to his expressing his legitimate feelings. At each session thereafter, he is asked to recount his experiences, whether successes or failures and, in case of the latter, corrective instruction is given.

It should be noted that the purpose of training in assertive behavior is to enable the person to behave effectively with other people. This is invariably true even if the expression of legitimate anger is involved. It is never meant to foster aggressiveness.

To illustrate the initiation of assertiveness training, let us take the example of an everyday situation that a man found difficult. Craig, a 27-year-old free-lance photographer, could not bring himself to request a waiter to take back overcooked food. The situation posed was that Craig had ordered a steak done rare, and it had arrived overdone. The conversation proceeded as follows:

Dr. W.: What would you do?
Craig: I wouldn't say anything to the waiter. I would feel irritated, but I'd eat the steak.

Dr. W.: Why would you not speak up to the waiter?
Craig: Because I wouldn't like to antagonize him.

Dr. W.: But you would be perfectly within your rights to do so. You have not got what you ordered and what you'll be paying for. You should ask him to take that steak back and bring you another, which he will probably do. If he *is* disagreeable, you should complain to the manager.

On the basis of such instructions, Craig gradually became more capable of expressing himself adequately. Each time he did so, the expression of his annoyance competitively decreased the fear and weakened its habit. Had we encountered difficulty, I might have play-acted the correct behavior with him. I would have taken the role of the waiter, and Craig would have "played himself" so that his errors could be corrected.

Assertiveness training has received some well-deserved publicity (and attention) in recent years, and is familiar to many people through workshops and do-it-yourself books. Such books may provide valuable help, especially through their practical examples, but many of them (e.g., Alberti and Emmons, 1978[2]; Fensterheim and Baer, 1975[3]) overlook the central role of social anxiety in timidity. Assertiveness training is effective because it opposes to anxiety competing emotions such as anger, affection, or admiration. Interaction with other people is the vehicle for the expression of the competing emotion. Occasionally a person without undue anxiety requires more effective social behavior, for example, pure behavior training. In encouraging assertive behavior while ignoring the social anxiety, the self-help books are missing the conceptual underpinnings even though the courses of action they suggest for their readers are generally effective. And they may overlook the frequently crucial subtleties of assertiveness training. The following case illustrates this.

PAULETTE, a young married woman, was, among other things, timid, so I had been teaching her the fundamentals of assertiveness. Though she had been successful with some people, she had made no progress where it was most important—with her husband. He was constantly criticizing her, but she was terrified of answering back because that would provoke further criticism. As a result, she had gone on passively enduring his verbal onslaughts.

We examined in detail her husband's way of criticizing her. The following incident was typical. While they were watching the evening news on television, he began criticizing the newscaster, a woman. Then he drew some parallels between the newscaster and his wife, and moved on to criticizing *her*. She responded (assertively, as she thought) by saying, "I'm just sick of this. You're always criticizing me and I wish you'd stop." This is the kind of statement that an assertiveness-training book might lead her to make. But it did not help. If anything, it encouraged him in his attitude. It emphasized his domination of the situation because she was, in effect, appealing to his sympathy; she was asking him to be nicer to her.

What was necessary, instead, was to change the general character of her approach to her husband's criticism. I advised Paulette to stop appealing to him and to address her remarks to *his* behavior. For example, she might say, "So you're at your favorite sport of spouting criticisms." That is a remark about *him*: she moves out of the role of the criticized and into the role of the critic. Although the content of the remark is important, what matters most is its direction. Its emotional tone is attack, not defense. It interrupts the flow of criticism, and it gives her a stronger and more spirited image—quite different from the old one of passive acceptance.

This example shows that even if a person has learned in general terms what assertive behavior is ("Stand up for yourself") he may not know how to apply it to a specific situation. Different kinds and nuances of assertion are called for by different circumstances, and it may take a skilled therapist to find out what needs to be done.

Illustrations of Assertiveness Training

COLLEEN, a 24-year-old stenographer, complained of chronic anxiety and a feeling of inadequacy in most of her social relationships, of which the most distressing was that with her mother-in-law. She also had phobic reactions to certain men, which, as I discovered, depended on how closely they resembled her father; and she reacted with fear to the ringing of the front doorbell or the sound of footsteps up the garden path. All these reactions stemmed from her early experiences with her father, who had terrorized her in her childhood in very many ways. He forbade her to have toys. One night when she was 8, he found a borrowed Raggedy Ann doll that she had hidden behind her dresser. He tore it to pieces in front of her. When she was 14, he removed her from school and had her work in one of his shops without pay. He would frequently creep up silently and pounce on her for not working hard enough. At 17, she ran away from home to marry a motor mechanic, with whom her relationship was generally happy.

Most of our treatment time was devoted to enabling her to stand up for herself in particular situations and to gain control of her relationships. She found it quite difficult in the beginning, so we began by having her assert herself with people unimportant to her. A parking-lot attendant was in the habit of making her park in the corner because he had a running joke about her used car. She had been going along with the joke, but was nevertheless upset by it.

She told him to stop joking at her expense, which he did, and she parked near the front of the lot, where she wanted to. She then began to assert herself with the superintendent of her apartment building, her neighbors who played music too loudly, and others. She overcame her anxieties and became self-reliant in all her dealings with other people, including her mother-in-law, her boss, and a client who resembled her father.

Finally, she deliberately made a trip of a thousand miles to see how she would do with her father himself. She experienced initial nervousness at their first encounter but after that was in complete control and comfortable throughout a three-week stay.

Therapy was unusually difficult; it took sixty-five sessions over two years. At its conclusion, Colleen described herself as having become a very well-adjusted and competent person. A year later, she reported that she was still going from strength to strength.

MARTHA, a fashion model of 28, was terribly upset over her current lover's indifference to her. Every one of many love affairs had followed the same pattern: she would first attract the man, and then, because she was afraid of not pleasing him, she would go to bed with him after the first or second date. She would behave in a very dependent way, phoning him several times a day, and invariably, after a time, the man would drop her.

Martha lacked assurance in dealing with other people, especially her mother, who was constantly pestering her because she wasn't married, and her boss. She was practically never free from feelings of tension and anxiety. She had had two years of psychoanalysis, and had come to me only because her analyst died. During the first few interviews, she repeatedly expressed doubt regarding the value of nonanalytic treatment.

At the fifth interview, when the counterproductiveness of her anxieties was made apparent to her and a plan for habit change was outlined, she began to feel optimistic. She was shown how to speak up for herself and avoid being obsequious toward her lover. He had recently asked to borrow $150 from her; Martha had agreed, even though she did not want to. We decided that she should say to him, "I've been thinking about it, and I'm not going to give you the money." She did this very calmly, without explanation or apology, and afterward had a feeling of triumph. Not long after, she ended the relationship with dignity and with relatively little upset. She began to feel more and more in control of her life.

Soon she found that for the first time she could express her own wishes in her sexual relationships. After her thirteenth interview, she went away on vacation and returned, six weeks later, to say that she was feeling more comfortable with other people and that she had enjoyed the new experience of being a social success. She no longer felt the need to have many dates as an assurance of her attractiveness. At the same time, she began to act more firmly with her mother. Instead of trying to defend herself against her mother's accusations, she would criticize the nagging, saying, for example, "Oh, yes. So here you go again with your fault-finding. Do you realize how boring you are when you nag . . . ?" Her mother, instead of becoming angry, as Martha had feared and expected, began to treat her in a more respectful and friendly way. Martha learned in similar fashion how to deal effectively with her boss.

Two months later, when she met a man who strongly attracted her, she acted with her new-found self-control and independence. After handling some difficulties very competently, she married him three months later. She had fourteen interviews in all, and a year later reported that she was happily married and well.

Assertiveness training progressed quite smoothly with Colleen and Martha, but this is not always the case. Anxiety from several sources may prevent successful assertiveness; it may be necessary to desensitize the individual before assertiveness training can begin. If, for instance, the person is afraid of the consequences of his behavior, of *what will happen if* he does take a stand, he may be unable to act assertively. The case of Charlie, a somewhat plump building inspector of 47, illustrates this. Charlie was unable to express his desires in general. He reported the following conversation, which he said was typical and which had occurred a short time before, just after he had finished lunch in a diner.

Waitress: What'll it be for dessert?
Charlie: Nothing, thank you. Just the check.

Waitress: Don't you want to try our cheesecake? We're famous for it.
Charlie: No, I'd really prefer not to. I'm on a diet.

Waitress: Just a little piece won't hurt. I'm telling you, you won't regret it.
Charlie: Well . . .

Waitress: I'll cut you just a thin slice and won't charge you much. How's that sound?
Charlie: Well, okay, I'll have some.

In fact, Charlie cannot stand cheesecake. The only reason that he ordered the dessert was that he was afraid of disappointing people. The more the waitress insisted, the more important he felt that it was to her, and the more pressure he felt to agree. It was because he was concerned about *what she might think* if he said no that he gave in to her. What is required in a case like this is, first, desensitizing the person to the imagined consequences of being assertive, and then moving on to the assertiveness training itself.

A second source of fear can be not the imagined consequences, but the person's feeling that when he speaks up, he seems pushy. The problem is not that he is worried about hurting someone else's feelings, he just fears the self-image of being pushy. In that case, he must first be convinced that he does *not*, in fact, seem pushy (that he is behaving, actually, like a human being with a sense of self-worth), and second, he may need to be desensitized to that image if the thought correction is not sufficient.

A third fear source is the circumstances surrounding the assertive act itself. A man at a tenants' meeting may be unable to give his opinion about renovations in the building, not because of what the others may think of him, but because the situation itself—speaking in front of a group of people—is too terrifying. He has, in other words, a useless fear of public speaking, or of being the center of attention. Assertiveness training cannot be carried out until he has lost his fear of being the center of attention.

This may be accomplished, again, by desensitization, or it may be greatly helped by a kind of play-acting called behavior rehearsal.

Two Examples of Behavior Rehearsal

GRETA, aged 26, a florist, dreaded the lash of her mother-in-law's tongue. The latter was critical of everything from Greta's cooking to her taste in furniture and the way she brought up her child. If the baby was playing on the floor, the mother-in-law would offer her opinion: "You shouldn't let the child crawl on the floor and pick up germs. It's dangerous." She had recently seen him playing with his penis and had warned Greta to spank him, because "if you let him play with his penis now, there'll be trouble later, and don't come running to me. Besides, it's just not right—he shouldn't do it."

Dr. W.: Let's pretend I'm your mother-in-law. I've just been criticizing you on the grounds that you don't train your child properly. Okay? I've just said it.

Greta: (Apologetically) I would probably say, "If you don't like the way I'm handling Billy, tell me what I'm doing wrong. I always . . ."

Dr. W.: I have to interrupt you. The way you're saying it is terribly defensive.

Greta: You're right.

Dr. W.: You must not do it that way. You could say, "On what basis do you make this remark?" Whatever the words— it's got to be a challenging statement that makes her account for her accusation. Now, let me hear you again.

Greta: Okay. "On what basis do you make this remark? Tell me if I'm doing something incorrect, then no doubt I'll correct it. If I feel that it's . . ."

Dr. W.: Don't make a speech, because that shows you're wriggling. In any case, you didn't stop with the challenge of your initial question. You went back to being defensive, which actually invites her to continue attacking you.

Greta: All right. "What grounds do you have for this accusation?"

Dr. W.: "Well, the child plays with his penis. No baby of mine would do that. I would smack his hand."

Greta: "Well, that doesn't disturb me in any way. It's normal behavior. I'm happy he's aware of things. There'll be no smacking of hands."

> *Dr. W.:*   That's much better. Actually, this is just the starting point. She's repeatedly doing this kind of thing to you. Well, now you've challenged her authority. You can go on from this to the general issue—"Look, Mother, I'm getting tired of your stream of baseless criticisms. I don't want to hear any comments unless you have a really good reason."

In the second example, a young woman's handling of unfair criticism by her father was used as practice material. The following dialogue took place after she had already learned the basics of assertiveness.

> JANICE, 24, an elementary school teacher, had left a message at her parents' home to say that she would not be there on Christmas Eve. When her father had called back, accusing her of having no deep feeling for her family, she had responded feebly and had been left very upset.

> *Dr. W.:*   What would you have liked to say?
>
> *Janice:*   I would have liked to say that I thought he was being unfair, that I have more feelings probably than anybody in the family. I was trying to do what I thought was best for everybody, and I didn't get the impression that my mother would be that disappointed if I didn't come up.
>
> *Dr. W.:*   That's rather bland and defensive. See if you can improve on it.
>
> *Janice:*   "I think you were exceptionally unfair in assuming that I did not want to come up and that I was the villain because I wasn't coming up to make the family happy."
>
> *Dr. W.:*   That response leaves you vulnerable. It is very unsatisfactory for you to complain to somebody that he is *unfair,* because if you do that, you're really in some sense putting yourself at his mercy. A better line of approach would be: "Your attack was absolutely unwarranted." In saying this, you are simply stating what you feel was wrong in his behavior. Now, do you think you could redo it?
>
> *Janice:*   How about "I don't think it was right for you to call me last night and say what you did, because you didn't have the facts straight. You should have checked with Mom first and be sure you understood the situation."
>
> *Dr. W.:*   That's much better.

Assertiveness training makes use of two of the change processes we noted in Chapter III. There is inhibition of anxiety by the competition of the anger, annoyance, affection, or whatever other emotion is relevant, and there is a rewarding of new ways of speaking and behaving. The reward is often of more than one kind—the achievement of control of a social relationship, getting the rare steak that one has ordered, and the approval that others (including the therapist) may express at one's display of backbone.

Sexual Inadequacy: Love Versus Anxiety

Anxiety has a special importance in human love life, for *it is the usual cause of sexual failures and difficulties in both sexes.* There are, of course, instances in which poor sexual responding is not due to anxiety, but to the simple fact that a *particular* partner does not sufficiently excite. The partner may lack physical attributes or mental abilities that are important, or the partner may not know how to stimulate sexually.

Anxiety, by contrast, impairs sexual responding in general, so that erotic responses to all partners are weakened. In men, the thought of failure is the usual cause of the fear; in women, it may be caused by many things, ranging from the mere sight of a penis to the belief that divine retribution is the wages of sexual pleasure. I have seen women who were overcome with guilt at the slightest sexual feeling toward men other than their husbands.

Male Sexual Fears

In men, inadequate sexual performance is usually due to fear of inadequate sexual performance. The anxiety either prevents or weakens penile erection or, much more commonly, produces premature ejaculation. A vicious circle develops: fear → failure → fear. Fear can have these effects only if it is *stronger* than the sexual excitation. The therapist therefore plans sexual exposures in which the sexual arousal is stronger than fear, the idea being that each time the fear is diminished by the competition of this arousal, the fear habit will be somewhat weakened. *It is important that the sexual arousal be at all times stronger than the fear to which it is opposed.* The therapist's first step is to ascertain at what point in the sexual approach anxiety begins and what factors increase it. Perhaps the man begins to feel anxious the moment he enters the bedroom; perhaps when he is lying naked in bed next to his partner.

The basic idea of the treatment is explained to him: he is to extend his sexual approach in slowly graded steps, never allowing himself to advance so far that he feels more than slight anxiety. If, for example, he feels a small amount of anxiety just lying in bed next to his wife, he is permitted to make no actual sexual approaches until the anxiety has entirely dissipated. This usually happens after two or three sessions. Then he can go on to the next stage—perhaps fondling her breasts, caressing her thighs, or lying on top of her without attempting entry. When this next step ceases to evoke anxiety, he may be permitted to move his penis against her clitoris. After this, he may be allowed a small degree of entry, and then increasing degrees — and then increasing movement. The precondition for advancing a stage is always the disappearance of all anxiety from the preceding stages.

The cooperation of the wife (or lover) is obviously critical to success. She must treat her husband's problem respectfully and lovingly, and not mock or goad him to achieve any particular level of performance.

The details of treatment naturally vary from person to person. An added procedure that is frequently of great value is to have the wife manipulate the penis to a point just short of ejaculation and then stop. After an interval, she does this again, and may repeat it several times. The effect is to lengthen the time to ejaculation so that after a number of sessions it may be half an hour or longer.

OSCAR, a 40-year-old architect, complained of premature ejaculations. At the age of 22, he had formed his first intimate association with a woman of his own age, with whom he had gotten along very well and had frequent and satisfying sexual intercourse. The association ended after three years, when he left to start his own practice in another town.

For years after this, he had only casual sexual affairs. Intercourse would at first last about a minute, but when he got to know a girl better, it would last as long as four minutes. Four years before I first saw him, when, after a prolonged abstinence, he attempted intercourse with a girl he had met at a party, he ejaculated before entry. Ever since, this had been his invariable reaction.

What brought him to treatment was that he had recently met Anne, a woman to whom he was so strongly attracted that he was for the first time in his life considering marriage. Although petting was frequent and passionate, his ejaculatory problem had made him resort to various excuses to avoid intercourse.

After explaining the role of anxiety and the general idea of using competing responses, I explained how the sexual situation itself, with Anne's cooperation, could solve his problem. To make that easier, he was to tell her that in the past he always had difficulty with intercourse after a long period of abstinence, and if she was patient with his gradual approach, they could look forward to successful intercourse.

Despite occasional errors through trying to press ahead too fast, the program succeeded very well. After two months of progress, they went away on vacation and had successful intercourse repeatedly. On their return, Oscar announced their intention of marrying the following month. Eight months later, he reported that the marriage was going well, with a sex life that was mutually satisfying.

Female Sexual Fears

Female sexual inadequacy is usually referred to by the obnoxious term "frigidity." In actuality, there is a wide range of difficulties—from a complete inability to be aroused, to a failure to have orgasms even when sexual excitement is very high.

While inadequate sexual response "across the board"—in relation to a wide range of partners—is the most serious problem, it is important to realize that a lack of response is often limited to a particular male, such as the woman's husband. The first question to be raised is what can be done to make him more acceptable. The solution may require changes in his general behavior—for example, showing greater consideration by calling when he is delayed at the office or taking a greater share in the household chores. Or maybe changes are needed in his modes of courtship and love play.

In a great many relationships, both parties may need to change because a spiral of mutual resentment has developed. The wife retaliates for the husband's excessive absorption in his work, perhaps by putting the children to bed so early that he cannot enjoy their company or by making sex hard for him to get. It is easy to see how such tactics can exacerbate negative feelings and behavior. The behavior therapist needs to identify the dynamics of these interactions and get the partners to agree to mutually desired changes in their behavior. The husband is asked to do certain things that his wife requests of him, such as coming home earlier from work and allowing more time for his family. In return, she lets the children stay up later so that he can be with them, and reduces the amount of time she spends watching television when he wants to be with her. In this way each has needs communicated and fulfilled, and so finds it easier and more enjoyable to do what the other requests. (This is another example of reward-based learning.) Programs of this kind are remarkably effective,[4] far more so than the venting of resentful feelings (which often merely makes things worse) that is widely encouraged in standard marital-counseling practice. Of course, mutual readjustments are not always successful. Some people are completely and unalterably wrong for each other.

When a woman's inhibition of sexual response is general, it is usually caused by anxiety. Previous experiences have attached feelings to sexual situations. Sometimes the relevant experience, which may date back many years, is outwardly trivial, like having been frightened in the act of masturbation, or there may be a grim history of sexual molestation, or a parent may have instilled the fear of God into the idea of sex.

Treatment naturally depends on the details of the case revealed by the therapist's analysis of it. (See Chapter VIII.) Where there has been faulty indoctrination, it is necessary to remove misconceptions about sex and provide reeducation. Where there is a useless fear habit based on emotional learning, some form of desensitization will probably be needed.

MARLENE was a 39-year-old guidance counselor, the mother of three children, who for many years had been happily married and had enjoyed excellent sexual relations with her husband. About seven years before, he had begun drinking increasingly, until drunkenness of varying degrees had become his customary state. Marlene was very much turned off by this change and found him more and more repulsive; before long, sexual contact with him became utterly repugnant. Nevertheless, she submitted to him at times but filed for divorce.

Both before the divorce and afterward, Marlene had a number of affairs, but she was distressed to find that, in contrast to the early years of her marriage, she was totally unable to have orgasms. She consulted me when she found this to be the case with a man with whom she had fallen deeply in love.

The behavior analysis revealed that the essence of the problem was a fear of being seen having an orgasm. She was easily able to have an orgasm masturbating in private. The treatment consisted of having her masturbate to orgasm with her lover standing closer and closer. First she did so in the dark, separated from him by the closed bathroom door. Subsequent approaches were based on bringing him closer and allowing more light. Her eventual ability to masturbate to orgasm openly while next to him proved, as expected. to be the bridge to her being able to resume having orgasms during intercourse.

Sometimes sexual difficulties can be treated by desensitization in the standard manner, using imagination, in the therapist's office.

NATALIE, a 27-year-old stage manager, needed treatment for both interpersonal anxiety and a profound distaste for sex. The former called for training in assertiveness, which she soon began to carry out effectively.

From an early age, she had often been darkly warned by her mother of the evil of sex. Those warnings had been confirmed by an attempted sexual assault by a middle-aged uncle about the time she reached puberty. Since her marriage five years previously, she had found sex unpleasant and had tried as much as possible to avoid it. Central to her problem was an aversion to the male sex organ.

In the attempt to overcome this by desensitization, I found that her picturing her husband's penis from any distance aroused more anxiety than could be mastered by relaxation. This difficulty was overcome by having her imagine looking at a nude male statue in a park, from a distance of thirty feet. After coming progressively closer to the statue, she could eventually calmly imagine herself handling the stone penis. The next series of scenes began with her at one end of her bedroom, seeing her nude husband's penis fifteen feet away. As desensitization proceeded, the penis was brought closer and closer.

Then she was asked to imagine that she quickly touched the penis — which made her anxious once again. With repetition, this image gradually stopped arousing anxiety, and then the duration of contact was increased. At the twentieth session, she said that she was enjoying sex and was having orgasms about 50 percent of the time.

VII

Two Special Methods of Therapy

The two methods that occupy this chapter have one thing in common: unlike the treatments so far described, they have very little to do with the treatment method used in animals. The first method deals with fears that are based on misinformation (see Chapter II). The second deals, like desensitization, with fears that are directly triggered by particular things, but it involves prolonged exposures to relatively strong anxiety, instead of desensitization's brief, weak exposures.

The Treatment of Fears Based on Wrong Beliefs

As will be further detailed in Chapter VIII, the fear triggers must be clearly identified before treatment can begin. Systematic desensitization is appropriate when a person is afraid of going into an elevator because he reacts automatically to enclosed spaces. It's not a suitable method if he is afraid because he believes that something terrible may really happen — that he may suffocate because the air would be exhausted if the elevator got stuck. If a fear is based on such a belief, the proper course is to correct the belief. To attempt to desensitize this person to elevators would be as futile as to try to desensitize him to a harmless garden snake if he believes it to be a dangerous animal. Nothing can induce him to insert his hand into the cage as long as he thinks the snake is poisonous.

In practice, overcoming a cognitively based fear consists of authoritatively challenging the patient's wrong beliefs by supplying corrective information. The presumed harmful consequences of situations or of the patient's own behavior must be shown to be nonexistent. I explain that a particular kind of snake or spider is not dangerous, that the pain in his chest does not mean heart disease, or that the social behavior of which he is ashamed is reasonable and acceptable. Such information may be reinforced by demonstrations or by reading, as befits the circumstances. It sometimes helps to use videotapes to show the patient that his view of his own behavior is erroneous; he can see, for instance, that he is not trembling at all as he speaks, even though he has assumed that he was. The fact that a chest pain is harmless may need to be supported by medical data such as an electrocardiogram; the dizziness and rapid heartbeat that an individual has found to precede a panic attack can become less threatening once it is demonstrated that it can be induced by hyperventilation.

Sometimes a person is easily disabused of the mistaken belief that has been causing anxiety.

KARRIE, aged 25, was a young mother who had developed a fear of throwing her baby off the balcony of her apartment. She was preoccupied with this thought during much of the day, and as a result she began to avoid the side of her apartment that was near the balcony. The idea was really that she might *lose control* of herself for a moment and throw the baby out.

I pointed out to her that she had never lost control before, that there was no reason to think that she might do so now, and that, in fact, she was suffering from a *fear* of doing it—a strongly *negative* reaction that actually made it less likely for her to do it than anyone who had not even thought about it. This argument erased the idea that she was in danger of losing control, and it thus eliminated the source of her fear.

Karrie was convinced in one session; there was a sense of revelation as she realized what had not occurred to her before. But it is often difficult to go against an idea that one has accepted for years. The person is used to his mistaken information, and it may take several sessions before he can be comfortable with the new idea that makes sense.

Some of the commonest fears of this kind are those having to do with illness.

SCOTT, a 43-year-old car dealer from Arkansas, was sitting in an office in New York City discussing a transaction when suddenly his face flushed, he felt short of breath, and he sensed a constriction in his chest. He became very anxious, thinking that he was about to die. His father and brother had both died of heart attacks, and his sister of high blood pressure. Scott went to a doctor that day for a complete checkup, which showed that he was in perfect health; yet he was left with the feeling that something was wrong. On the plane back to Arkansas the next day, he felt the need to have someone with him in case the attack recurred. From then on, he was continuously anxious whenever he was alone.

When I first saw Scott, this fear, which had had its roots in his anxiety over physical symptoms, had been with him for five years. I began by carefully explaining to him that those symptoms were typical of a kind of very rapid beating of the heart that occurs in normal people. It starts suddenly, stops just as suddenly after minutes or hours, and produces strange sensations like those he had experienced. While it is an unusual state of heart function, it is not harmful. It took six sessions and the help of medical textbooks to convince him that he was in no danger. Through losing his fear of heart attacks, he lost his fear of being alone.

LYDIA, a 60-year-old newspaper editor, had an obsessional fear of cancer that had lasted twenty years. She had tried various remedies, including psychoanalysis and insulin-shock treatment, none of which had had any effect. When she was 17, her parents persuaded her to marry a man of "good family" to whom she was not attracted, who was not as bright as she, but who was well-meaning. The marriage was an emotional disaster, and she had a strong desire to leave him. She was unable to do so, though, because she was afraid that her parents would disapprove. As time went on, the anxiety caused by this conflict increased. She described "terrible depressions and attacks of panic."

When she was 51, she had a hysterectomy for benign tumors of the uterus. On waking from the anesthesia, she asked the nurse, "Did I have cancer or didn't I?" The nurse replied, "A friend of mine had cancer and lived to be seventy." Lydia was terrified. The surgeon showed her reports that the tumors were not malignant, but she was unconvinced. She began probing for cancers, especially in her breasts, and then, as time passed, she moved to examining other parts of her body at the slightest provocation. For example, when she noticed blood on her toothbrush after brushing her teeth, she concluded that she had cancer of the mouth and went into a panic. At the time she came to see me, she was obsessed with the thought that she had cancer of the intestines. She scrutinized her bowel movements; any slight diarrhea or constipation made her think that she had developed cancer of the bowel. She was under the impression that cancer could develop in a day or a week; consequently, she had had many X rays and other examinations, none of which showed any sign of cancer.

Realizing that it was her wrong thinking that had to be changed, I presented her with evidence from medical articles indicating that cancer of the bowel takes a year to double its size. She had just been examined with a medical instrument that enables a doctor to examine precisely the bowel wall. "If," I reasoned with her, "you have cancer of the bowel now that is so small that it cannot be seen with this instrument, it will still be of negligible size a year from now. Even then it may be too small to be detected. And a cancer of the bowel that small cannot produce diarrhea or any other symptoms. So cancer is the one thing that cannot be the cause. A once-a-year checkup with this instrument is more than enough." This argument, repeated over several sessions, was sufficient to convince her. (Her social fears also had to be treated by a combination of assertiveness training and systematic desensitization.)

It is often not enough just to reason with someone: a person may accept an idea more readily if he can experience it directly. An activity in which he participates can play a vital role in changing what he perceives to be the source of his fear. The activity may be quite elaborate, as illustrated in the case of Darryl.

DARRYL, a 35-year-old typesetter who lived in St. Louis, had developed a fear of rabies. It was aroused by any nick or scratch in his skin. Two months before he came to see me, his fear had become much worse when he read about a child who was bitten by a bat during the day, and who died from the bite. Because he knew that bats fly most often after dark, Darryl was afraid to go to sleep at night. He blocked the chimney and locked all the doors and windows, but, since reading about the boy, he was reluctant to go out even during the day.

His fear had begun two years earlier, when he was trying to scare off some tom cats in an alley behind his house. They had scratched his arm in several places, so he had gone to see a doctor. The doctor asked him "Do you reckon that the cats may be rabid?" He answered that he didn't think so, but that he wasn't sure. He felt a mild fear that, as he began to think about it over the next few days, became progressively stronger. By the end of a month, it reached a level of panic, and Darryl had become afraid of touching things, especially sharp objects. The doctor then sent him to a psychiatrist, who tried various drugs that enabled him to touch an increased number of things. The psychiatrist also suggested that he go to live with a friend, rather than living alone. Darryl remarked that there might be bats in his friend's house, at which point the psychiatrist said, "Well, bats *are* notorious for rabies." From that time on, Darryl's preoccupation with bats had been ceaseless.

Since Darryl's fear was due to his gross overestimation of the danger of getting rabies, I first tried to convince him—by reference to statistics—that it was highly unlikely that he would be attacked by a rabid animal. But he argued that there was always a *possibility*, however remote. And in the end he was right; there *was* always a possibility. It was so small, though, that it certainly did not justify his ruining his life in order to prevent it.

I therefore devised an unusual strategy. I had to convince Darryl that he had an impregnable defense against rabies. There was, at the time that he came to see me, a vaccine available, although it was painful and only temporarily effective. (Since then, a more lasting and relatively painless vaccine has been developed.) I asked him if he would be willing to put up with the discomfort of vaccination, as well as occasional visits for painful booster shots, in order to become free of his fear. He thought it over for a few days and then decided that any momentary pain would be insignificant if his obsession could be ended and his life returned to normal.

I felt it desirable to introduce this vaccine to him as vividly as possible, since his previous experiences with doctors had rendered him somewhat distrustful. Therefore, I ordered laboratory studies that are not ordinarily required for the administration of vaccines. In cooperation with the university's laboratories, we did some blood tests and went ahead with the vaccination. Two days later, we again took blood samples and these showed that the vaccination had "taken," and that Darryl was resistant to rabies. I showed Darryl the complete lab reports, and upon reading them himself he felt much better.

I then telephoned Darryl's doctor in St. Louis and explained the situation to him; he was happy to provide Darryl with booster vaccines as often as necessary. Once Darryl realized that he had nothing to fear from rabies (no matter how remote the possibility), his fear was overcome and his obsession ended.

Darryl's fear based on information was overcome by new information—that he had become immune to rabies. Even though he had never been bitten by a rabid animal and probably never would be, he now felt secure in the knowledge that he was invulnerable. And since it was knowledge that had been at the source of his fear, knowledge was sufficient to cure him. His participation in the complete vaccination procedure (the taking of blood tests before and after, the vaccination itself, the reading of blood test results) allowed Darryl to experience intensely the events that effected the crucial change in him. The case is a dramatic illustration of the enormous power of belief, first in causing a severe useless fear, and then in overcoming that fear.

Sometimes a circuit develops between misinformation and the fear that is based on it. In this case, a technique called *thought-stopping* is used to interrupt the circuit.

> NORMAN was a 46-year-old TV repairman who was afraid that he had been responsible for killing a girl whose murder had some years ago been reported in the news. His fear persisted even after he had read and reread reports that the killer had been apprehended, had confessed guilt, and had been sentenced to a long prison term.
>
> Norman had at the time of the crime been an alcoholic, so he feared that he had done the deed during a blackout under the influence. The anxiety caused him to avoid any situation where he might encounter a young girl. He even refused to see his granddaughter. If he drove past an elementary school, he sometimes did not stop at the traffic light for fear that if he did, he might molest one of the girls. In addition, he began elaborate rituals of checking in closets, creeks, lockers, trunks, and other places to ensure that he had not left a dead or mutilated body in them.

The behavior analysis revealed that there was indeed a continuous connection between his thinking and fear habits: the thought would occur that he had killed the girl, this would make him anxious, and the more anxious he became, the more the thought occurred to him. Treatment involved the thought-stopping technique. Norman was taught the habit of instantly switching his thoughts to something else whenever the crime image arose. With practice, he could automatically block the thought at its beginning; eventually, he stopped having it at all. He had a variety of related fears that had to be dealt with in other ways. For example, he was afraid that he might poison people with sulfuric acid by touching them after he had been in contact with a car battery or a battery cable. This was treated by the flooding method described on the following pages.

Intense Fear Exposure (Flooding)

The reader who has read all that has gone before in this book will probably be surprised to learn that a behavioral treatment exists that seems to be the very opposite of desensitization. It is called flooding, and consists of *exposing the individual to relatively strong anxiety for prolonged periods*—up to an hour and sometimes more. What typically happens is this: The person feels a certain level of anxiety—say, 50 units—when he is briefly exposed to a particular situation. If he is exposed to that situation over an extended time, his level may rise to 85. It then decreases of its own accord to 25 or 35, where it levels off. The procedure is repeated at subsequent sessions until the level reaches zero. Norman, for example, was required to engage in normal daily activities while "contaminated" with corrosion from car battery terminals. After touching these, he would touch other people, go to restaurants and shops, visit friends, and so forth, so that he could contaminate large numbers of people. This raised his anxiety to a high level—as though he were "flooded" with anxiety—and then over an extended time it diminished. After repeating this several times over the course of a few weeks, Norman lost his concern with contamination by battery acid.

The first reported case of flooding, in 1938, was of a young girl who was afraid of being in automobiles. Her doctor, perhaps impulsively attempting a "sink or swim" method for overcoming her fear, ordered that she be driven from her home to his New York office. The trip involved a drive of about an hour and a half, and included crossing several bridges and going through the Holland Tunnel, both of which made her especially anxious. On the morning of the ride, before she left home, she was in a state of panic. She was violently nauseated and felt faint. Her anxiety continued during most of the ride, but as she approached her physician's office, it subsided. It was much weaker on the return trip and gradually diminished on subsequent occasions when she was in the car.

The first technical description of the method of flooding was provided by a British physician, Dr. Nicholas Malleson.[1] One of his patients was an Indian student who was mortally afraid of college examinations because of the terrible consequences that he thought would follow if he were to fail: derision from his colleagues in India, the disappointment of his family, and financial loss. The treatment consisted of having him imagine as vividly as possible that the consequences of failure were actually happening: the fingers of scorn pointed at him, his wife and mother in tears. At first, as he followed the instructions, his sobbings increased, but after a while they diminished. It became more and more difficult for him to maintain vivid images, and at the same time the emotion began to ebb. Within half an hour he was calm. The treatment was repeated twice a day during the next two days before his examination, and by the time the examination came, he reported himself almost totally unable to feel frightened. He passed without difficulty.

In modern flooding techniques, the therapist arranges for the person to be exposed to relatively strong fear situations. These situations, whether real or imagined, are presented continuously. The presentation lasts until the anxiety begins to wane, which under normal circumstances takes between ten minutes and an hour. If the flooding is successful, the amount of anxiety experienced in relation to that situation will be less at the end of the session, and also at the next session. The anxiety habit is weakened.

It is not understood precisely how flooding works; what is important is that it does work in many cases. There are two observations that may shed some light on the process. The first involves what Pavlov called *protective inhibition.* He observed that if a sound elicits an emotional response, then increasing its loudness or duration increases the response. But at a certain degree of loudness or after a certain length of time, the response *diminishes* instead of increasing. He thought this due to a built-in mechanism of inhibition that protects the individual from too much excitation.

The second observation is related to the presence of the therapist. Flooding that is done when the therapist is present is much more likely to be beneficial than flooding carried out by the individual alone. Perhaps this is because of emotional competition brought about by the presence of the therapist. It is possible that this is why, in the case of the girl who was afraid to be inside a car, she began to feel better as she drew near her doctor's office.

Flooding has been widely used in recent years in the treatment of a variety of phobias. Although its success has been considerable, it has not, with a few exceptions, equaled that of desensitization. Moreover, it is *stressful,* and that makes it undesirable in comparison with desensitization. The stress can be so severe that some people are unwilling to continue treatment.

However, there is one kind of neurotic patient for whom flooding has distinctly brightened the outlook and for whom it is today, without doubt, the most effective treatment. This is the obsessional person who, like Norman, spends much of his time avoiding and washing "contaminations" from his hands and performing rituals that ward off the effects of the contamination. Such people have for decades been the despair of psychiatrists. In the past twenty-five years, desensitization was often effective, but it was almost always very time-consuming. Flooding, by contrast, results in significant and lasting improvements in about 70 percent of these cases in a matter of weeks.

The following account of the treatment of such a case is typical.

CELIA was a single girl of 20 years of age. For the past two years, she had been preoccupied with avoiding and removing "contamination" by people or things that had in some way been associated with a college she had attended. She had always regarded this college as beneath her, since she never worked very hard in high school, and her ability would have led her to a much more prestigious school if her grades had been better.

Her obsession began after an excruciating experience. Celia's roommate had a friend named Grace, whom Celia found disgusting because she rarely washed herself or her clothes. One evening, Celia returned to her room to find the other two girls there. Grace was lying on Celia's bed, describing a drunken sexual experience. While Grace was talking, Celia noticed lice crawling in her hair. This revolting sight confirmed Celia's distaste for the school and its students. Whereas previously she had kept aloof from the other students, she now began to avoid touching them or any objects they might have touched. She had her roommate move from the room and tried to exclude everyone else. If someone did enter, she would throw out any small objects that person had handled, such as a pencil or paper. She washed the floor, the furniture, and any clothing the visitor might have touched.

Before Celia decided to have behavior therapy, she tried a succession of conventional treatments, including lengthy hospitalizations. After the behavior analysis was done, I attempted to treat her by having her imagine contaminations, but without success. I then decided on flooding, using real objects. I requested her parents to send various articles she had used while at college, and received a package containing clothing, written materials, and books. At her next visit, Celia was given a careful description of the flooding technique.

She was then conducted into a colleague's office on the desk of which were arranged the articles sent by her parents. After she had been assured that she would not be required to do anything against her will, she was asked to list these articles in increasing order of the discomfort she would expect to have on contact. My colleague then held up a pencil, which she had listed as the least anxiety-evoking, and asked her to do the same, but she adamantly refused. He placed his hand on the desk and, as Celia watched, moved it closer to the pencil, finally touching it with the tips of his fingers. Next, he gingerly lifted it from the table, held it more firmly, and, at last, wrote with it. None of this bothered her. Then he asked her if she would mind copying what he had just done. For two sessions, she was too afraid to do this, but at the third she was able to touch and handle the pencil as he had done.

This was the beginning of the flooding, for the contact made her feel contaminated and therefore anxious. In order to maintain the exposure of the contamination, *she was asked to refrain from washing for two hours*. During this period, her distress progressively diminished to a low level, and then she was allowed to wash.

In the course of the next few sessions, Celia came to be able to touch and use all the objects and wear all the clothing for increasing periods, and eventually for the duration of an entire afternoon without washing.

The success of the treatment was gratifying. Under further guidance, Celia exposed herself to many things: touching people, walls and doorknobs, and books. After several weeks, she returned to her parents' home, and six weeks later entered a prestigious college. Followed up at intervals during the next three years, she reported that the last vestiges of her obsession had disappeared.

Flooding is a relatively new technique, but it may be related to a phenomenon called *abreaction,* which has been known for centuries. In abreaction, an individual recounts a very disturbing event associated with the onset of his fear. As he does so, he becomes tremendously emotional and seems to be reliving the experience. Sometimes he is much improved after going through this process.

Abreaction does not very often occur, and when it does, it is usually unexpected. A truck driver developed a fear of driving his truck after an accident—his truck had hit an oil slick, spun around, and slammed into a partition. He had fallen into some bushes, and so had luckily escaped injury, but he had been left with the fear of driving. After the usual history-taking and other preliminary steps, I began to desensitize him. In the first scene, he imagined that he was approaching the door of a parked car and reaching for the handle. The moment he formed that scene, he burst into a vivid and excited description of the accident in his truck. He became very upset as he relived the experience and was able to calm down only after several minutes. Remarkably, his fear was gone after that. He needed no other treatment, and in fact was able to resume work the next day!

There is no really reliable way to bring on an abreaction, and the fact that this "reliving" may occur in a person does not mean that he will necessarily benefit from it. It may not change him at all; occasionally, it may even make him worse.

Thus, abreaction is less controllable and less successful than its modern cousin, flooding.

Before a therapist can use any of the treatment methods that have been outlined in the last three chapters, he must know precisely what the triggers are to the patient's useless fears. How this knowledge is obtained is described in the next chapter.

VIII

Behavior Analysis:
Why Expert Help Is Necessary

We have seen the various ways in which a person may be plunged into the caldron of neurosis, and we have surveyed the methods that may extricate him. But every person is unique, and there is endless variety in the structure of neurotic problems. Effective treatment depends on determining the exact relationship between specific events and the individual's reactions to those events. This assessment, which we will call *behavior analysis.,* is the most critical task in behavior therapy, and calls for the highest skill and diligence. The fact that it is necessary is the main reason that do-it-yourself manuals are of limited value.

The information used in treatment comes for the most part from what the person says. Most people are willingly communicative, but some unwittingly mislead the therapist in important matters. Sometimes a person is not fully aware of some aspects of his experiences. Sometimes he is simply inaccurate in the recounting. Sometimes he omits or slants information because of embarrassment, or he distorts the picture because he has his own "understanding" of the problem. Alice, whom we shall meet in the next chapter, wrongly attributed the onset of her severe useless fears to the anesthetic used during an operation she had undergone. Close questioning showed beyond doubt that social stresses were their actual cause and that the anesthetic was incidental. The treatments that would follow from the two explanations are, as may be expected, very different.

If skilled questioning by the therapist does not enable the person to relate his anxiety to anything, it may be that the anxiety has an organic cause. That is, it is physiologically based—perhaps on an overactive thyroid condition or other hormonal abnormalities. Organic anxiety is usually more or less continuous and is not altered by learning. Occasionally, though, a person may have a *learned* anxiety (a useless fear) that is more or less continuous but is not related to a particular situation—so-called free-floating anxiety.

The behavior analysis is carried out to determine the precise nature of the problem. At the first interview, the person is asked to state the difficulties that have brought him to treatment. The history of each complaint is traced from its onset, with special attention given to any circumstances that may have made it better or worse. Anxiety is most often the main presenting complaint, but even when it is not, careful probing reveals the central role it has in almost every neurotic problem. The factors that presently control the anxiety reactions are examined with particular care.

The therapist then turns his attention to the person's background in order to gain a general perspective as well as some examples of how the patient has responded to a variety of situations and relationships. The background information may also reveal new aspects of the problems at hand. The probing starts with his early home life. Some of the questions asked include: How did you perceive your parents? How did they relate to each other? Were they kind and interested in you? What were their reasons for, and methods of, punishment? How much religious training did they instill? Does it still directly influence your life? How did you relate to your brothers and sisters? Did you have any childhood fears or nervous thoughts?

With regard to educational life: Did you like school? How successful were you, scholastically and at sports? Did you make friends? Did anyone bully you? When did you leave school, and what did you then do? How did you get along in each subsequent educational or occupational setting?

The history concludes with the person's love life: How old were you when you first had sexual feelings? In what contexts did they arise? Did you masturbate, and did this produce feelings of guilt or thoughts of dreadful consequences? At what age did you begin heterosexual (or homosexual) relationships? When and with whom did you have emotionally important relationships, and how did each work out? In respect to each relationship, what attracted you to your partner? How did you get along, and how satisfactory was the sexual side of the relationship? The aspects of love and emotional warmth are often more important than sexual behavior as such.

Finally, the person answers several questionnaires that have been found helpful. One of these, the Willoughby Questionnaire,[1] provides a measure of the range and severity of neurotic reactions, especially in relation to social situations. High-scoring responses to particular questions indicate a need for detailed probing in those areas. For example, if the answers show great sensitivity to criticism, the therapist will explore how this sensitivity is related to the control of the criticism and the identity of the critic.

An indispensable feature of the questioning is the permissive, anxiety-countering attitude of the therapist. He makes no criticism of the patient and goes out of his way to correct any unjustified self-criticisms.

The following excerpts are from the first interview with Carol, a 21-year-old x-ray technician with social fears.

Dr. W.:   What brings you here?
Carol: I am very nervous all the time.

Dr. W.:   How long has this been so?
Carol: Since I was about 14.

Dr. W.:   Are you saying that before you were 14 you were not nervous?
Carol: Well, I was, but not to this extreme. Even in elementary school when I'd have to read something in front of the class, I'd get very nervous about it.

Dr. W.:   What happened at 14 that made you nervous?
Carol: When I was in seventh grade I had to read something in front of the class.

Dr. W.:   Yes?
Carol: I was holding the paper and I started shaking. The teacher said, "What's the matter?" and I couldn't talk. From then on, if I had to read something, I'd put it down on the desk and stare at it. I'd be too nervous to read it.

Dr. W.:   So after this incident you were much worse?
Carol: Yes. In high school I wouldn't sleep for nights, worrying about giving a speech in front of class.

Dr. W.:   What about outside school?
Carol: I was afraid when I went out with boys. Especially if I would have a blind date, I'd be scared to death.

Dr. W.:   And if you went out with somebody you knew?
Carol: Well, after a while I'd be a little calmer, but still nervous.

Dr. W.:   And what if you went out with girlfriends?
Carol: Not as much.

Dr. W.:   When did you graduate from school?
Carol: Four years ago.

Dr. W.:   And what did you do then?
Carol: I became an X-ray technician.

Dr. W.:   Do you like this work?
Carol: Not really. I thought it was interesting, but once I got there I was very nervous about everything. It would scare me to be with patients.

Dr. W.:   During the four years that you've been doing this work, have you become more nervous, or less nervous, or stayed the same?
Carol: Definitely more.

Dr. W.:   Do patients still make you nervous?
Carol: And my boss.

Dr. W.:   Yes?
Carol: He makes me extremely nervous. I'm afraid of him.

Dr. W.:   Why? Does he carry on? Does he scream and so on?
Carol: Never at me. But I'm always afraid that it will happen.

Dr. W.:   I see. And who else scares you?
Carol: Men. If I go out with them.

Dr. W.:   What about men who come in where you are working, like medical students?
Carol: Yes, they scare me too.

Dr. W.:   They scare you? How?
Carol: I'm just afraid of how I'll act—that my nervousness will show through.

Dr. W.:   Well, that's while you're at work. Does anything scare you when you're away from work?
Carol: Just going out. I'm afraid, you know, that they'll see the way I am. I'm afraid to pick something up, because I'm afraid that I'm going to shake, and my mouth is all tightened up. I'm afraid to look at people directly in the eye.

Dr. W.:   Are you only afraid of looking in the eye the person who is with you, or anybody?
Carol: Anybody.

Dr. W.:   So looking at a person face to face increases your nervousness?
Carol: Yes.

Dr. W.:   Suppose that you're walking down the street and there's a bench across the road with some people waiting for a bus. Those people are vaguely looking across the street. Are you aware of their presence?

Carol: Yes, definitely.

Dr. W.:   Even though they may not be particularly looking at you?

Carol: Yes.

Dr. W.:   Now, supposing we take people away altogether. Suppose that you were just walking all by yourself, say, in a park. There is no one else at all there. Are you then completely comfortable?

Carol: Yes.

Dr. W.:   Well, what about people at home?

Carol: No, it doesn't bother me at home.

Dr. W.:   Your mother can look at you as much as she likes?

Carol: Yes, it's really silly but . . .

Dr. W.:   It's not silly. It's just the way things have developed.

Carol: Yes, I know.

Dr. W.:   And who else can look at you without bothering you?

Carol: My whole family.

Dr. W.:   Who is in your family?

Carol: My father, mother, my sister, my grandmother.

Dr. W.:   Besides these people, are there any others at all who can look at you without disturbing you?

Carol: No.

Dr. W.:   What about a little baby?

Carol: No, that doesn't disturb me, nor an older person who is senile or something.

Dr. W.:   What about a boy of 4?

Carol: No. It's when they get to their teens.

Dr. W.:   At what age do children begin to bother you?

Carol: Around in their teens.

Dr. W.:   I take it that a boy of 12 wouldn't be as bad as one of 18.

Carol: No.

The foregoing illustrates the care that is taken to establish the precise details of the situations that are disturbing. I learned from the questioning that this young woman had, since the age of 14, been excessively anxious under the scrutiny of strangers; more if performing before them in some way. Her sensitivity had increased over the years, so that she was now anxious even when she felt herself watched in the most casual way; for example, while walking down the street. She was more affected by men than by women, especially when there were erotic overtones. Anxiety was further raised by eye contact. The only people under whose gaze she was comfortable were members of her own family, very young children, and old people. There was a clear relationship between the other person's age and the intensity of her distress.

Other areas of needless anxiety were revealed in further interviews, such as an oversensitivity to criticism. These were examined with similar care. Meanwhile, it is important to note that Carol's initial statement that she was very nervous "all the time" was quite an exaggeration; she did not have free-floating anxiety.

The treatment that would normally be used for the fear of being looked at by strangers is systematic desensitization, but since I myself was a stranger, my very presence would raise her anxiety. Standard desensitization was therefore not feasible. In a case like Carol's, the therapist would tape-record descriptions of increasingly upsetting scenes. He would also teach the patient how to relax in progressive stages. At home, the patient would relax and play each recorded scene description again and again until it ceased to distress her. She would do this with each scene in succession in ascending order of disturbance.

Initial Analysis in a Fear of Fainting

Eileen was a 40-year-old housewife whose life was dominated by a fear of fainting. The factors controlling the fear were uncovered during the following interview. Also revealed were social fears that were related to the fear of fainting. (Other unrelated useless fears were also found in later interviews.)

Dr. W.:   What is your difficulty?
Eileen: A fear of passing out.

Dr. W.:   How long have you had this fear?
Eileen: Since I was 17.

Dr. W.:   Have you ever passed out?
Eileen: No. That's the silly thing. Never have.

Dr. W.:   Can you remember how this began?
Eileen: The first incident—when I was 17—was in church at an Easter service. I felt very dizzy and left the service, and after that I was just afraid that it would recur. I remember my parents took me to the family doctor, but he never really

found anything wrong after a lot of testing. Finally it was diagnosed that my tonsils were causing inner ear problems. I had the tonsils removed, but continued to have that fear.

Dr. W.:   Do you have this fear of passing out all the time?

Eileen: Not wholly. If I'm in a church or a meeting, I always make sure that I'm near a door.

Dr. W.:   Well, then, does this mean that it's only in public situations, like being in a church?

Eileen: Generally, yes.

Dr. W.:   You don't have the fear of passing out when you're at home?

Eileen: No.

Dr. W.:   What about when you're at the homes of your friends?

Eileen: I play bridge at homes of friends quite a bit and sometimes I am uncomfortable.

Dr. W.:   What are the times?

Eileen: I don't know how to differentiate them.

Dr. W.:   Can you point to any circumstances that might occur at the homes of your friends that would make you uncomfortable?

Eileen: Not really.

Dr. W.:   Well, how do you imagine this passing out would happen?

Eileen: Since I never have, it's hard to imagine. Occasionally I have a weak feeling and my knees start to shake a little bit and my hands perspire.

Dr. W.:   And what do you think could happen after that?

Eileen: I don't really know. I guess just drop over. I've just been thinking about how it could have started. And I remember when I was 5 I had an eye operation. In those days the parents weren't allowed in the hospital. You weren't told about it beforehand.

Dr. W.:   Uh-huh.

Eileen: I remember being dropped off at the hospital very frightened, and a few hours later a boy saying, "Oh, that gown means you're going to have surgery." And then I very vividly remember the ether. And it's that feeling sometimes. I refused anesthetics, even when I had my four children.

Dr. W.:   Well, what was the effect on you when the boy said you were going to have surgery?

Eileen: Total terror. You know, in those days there was no shot before you went up into the room.

Dr. W.: When they dropped you at the hospital, didn't they tell you that you were going to have an operation?

Eileen: No.

Dr. W.: When the boy told you, you had total terror?

Eileen: Yes.

Dr. W.: So, when exactly did you have the total terror?

Eileen: Being in the anesthetic room. I remember bottles on the wall, and then being told to breathe into something.

Dr. W.: Did you struggle?

Eileen: I don't know.

Dr. W.: Did I correctly hear that you recall that experience as in some way similar to the feeling that you get nowadays?

Eileen: Yes.

Dr. W.: In what respects?

Eileen: It's a feeling of turning to ice, a slight dizziness. Sounds getting louder maybe.

Dr. W.: You said a few minutes ago that sometimes you have a kind of beginning reaction—your knees shake, your hands perspire.

Eileen: Yes.

Dr. W.: What other feelings do you have?

Eileen: A lightheaded feeling.

Dr. W.: Well, is it that which has some similarity to this terror experience when you were 5? Or what?

Eileen: Yes. It's not just dizzy; it's a feeling of things going up and down. I don't know how to explain it.

Dr. W.: Okay. Now on this occasion when you were 17 you had dizziness at the Easter service?

Eileen: Yes.

Dr. W.: When have you had dizziness again?

Eileen: Just in some of these public situations.

Dr. W.: You mean if you go into a crowded room you'll become dizzy?

Eileen: Yes. But if I'm near a door, I'm fine.

Dr. W.: Is it when you become dizzy that you think that you may lose consciousness?

Eileen: Yes.

Dr. W.:   Do you ever feel fearful without feeling dizzy?

Eileen: Oh yes. Every morning when I think of my schedule for the day.

Dr. W.:   Uh-huh.

Eileen: Isn't that silly?

Dr. W.:   No. It's just your habit. When you think of your schedule for the day, what are you really thinking about? Is it the possible situations that may, in a sense, endanger you?

Eileen: Right. Exactly.

Dr. W.:   Can you suggest what there is about a crowd that makes it particularly dangerous from this point of view?

Eileen: Just no way of ready escape.

Dr. W.:   Besides crowds, are there any other fearful situations?

Eileen: Oh, sometimes driving, car-pooling with neighbors when I'm taking the children places. I'm fine in the car alone.

Dr. W.:   In those situations do you ever have the fear that you might lose consciousness?

Eileen: Yes.

Dr. W.:   Any other situations?

Eileen: In our swim club with a lot of people around and diving.

Dr. W.:   Do you then also think that you might lose consciousness?

Eileen: Yes, there again.

Dr. W.:   Is this fear of passing out the only important problem in your life?

Eileen: I would say so.

Dr. W.:   What if that problem was taken away?

Eileen: Oh, it would be wonderful.

It was clear that Eileen really had two fears. In the first place, she had a fear of crowds or, more exactly, a fear related to the proximity of people outside her own family—the more of them, the worse. She felt better near a door, since she could escape. In the second place, this fear included a number of symptoms, especially dizziness, that suggested the threat of losing consciousness, which was in itself upsetting. It later emerged that Eileen was also fearful of the possibility of being seen to be unconscious (or helpless in any other way) in the presence of strangers. In contrast to Alice (see "A Case of Anxiety and Depression," in Chapter IX), an anesthethic experience really was relevant to Eileen's anxiety reactions.

In further interviews, the usual wide exploratory net was spread and some other areas of useless fear were identified; for example, the sight of injuries or of other people's fainting. Systematic desensitization was the treatment used in all areas, and her recovery was virtually complete in sixteen sessions, when therapy was ended. Four months later, Eileen wrote that certain activities had, since her treatment, become completely easy for the first time. Among these were driving children to wherever they needed to go, regardless of the amount of traffic or the number of delays at traffic lights; shopping for food without her husband; walking instead of driving to nearby stores; and going out to dinner or ball games. She still experienced slight fear when shopping in large department stores and attending large school meetings. A year later, she reported that she was quite untroubled by any of the old concerns; this is not surprising, since the remaining fears were weak enough to be successfully competed with by emotions aroused in the life situations.

Some Complexities of Behavior Analysis

In the interviews with Carol and Eileen, what we saw was how sources or triggers of anxiety were given definition. The general areas had been accurately provided by each woman in the first place. In many cases, however, the true sources of the fear or other behavioral disturbance are quite different from those which the person initially presents. A fear that is aroused in a particular context *may be caused not by that context,* but by something associated with it. What someone says is a fear of flying may really be a fear of the *confinement* of a plane—a fear that will probably also arise in other confined situations, such as elevators or small rooms. Loneliness, similarly, may turn out not to be fearful in itself, but merely the setting for the true source of the fear—fear of silence, say, or the possibility of intruders.

It is not always physical similarity that leads to fear triggers being grouped together in the same hierarchy. Sometimes they are in the same grouping not because of a common feature like height or color but because they elicit the same feeling. The sense of enclosure mentioned above was produced in one person by being in a small room, by irremovable fingernail polish, or by lying in a tightly made bed. These three things are physically dissimilar, but each gives rise to a feeling of constriction, which then causes the anxiety. The person is thus responding with anxiety to his own feeling of constriction, not directly to the outside world.

With certain kinds of fears, it is usual for the true source of anxiety to be obscured. Agoraphobia, or "housewives' disease," is a good example. The Greek word *agoraphobia* means fear of the marketplace. Agoraphobia is more broadly defined as fear of open spaces, but it very commonly also involves fear of separation from a "safe" person. The individual is fearful in relation to the *degree* of his separation from the safe place, usually his own home, or a safe person, usually the spouse. (Sometimes there are a number of safe people, usually relations and friends.) If the therapist accepted the fears at face value, he would be desensitizing the patient to increasing separation in time and space. The therapist would make an attempt to break down the fear by having the deeply relaxed person imagine, for example, being separated from his house by five yards, then ten yards, then twenty yards, and so on. The truth is that this would not often succeed, since only 10 or 15 percent of agoraphobias are primarily fears of separation.

In most cases of agoraphobia, investigation shows the real basis of the fear to be elsewhere. For instance, we may find that the person is unrealistically afraid of some physical catastrophe, such as a heart attack, which comes to his mind whenever he feels a pain in his chest. The reason he is afraid to be far from home is that if the pain were to arise, he would not be able to summon help immediately. Obviously, to treat this person's fear of space by desensitizing him to gradually increasing imagined distances away from home would miss the point. He *is* afraid of being away from home, but only as a secondary matter. Therapy must be directed to the attacks of chest pain. He must first be convinced that he has no heart or chest disease; if he still has anxiety reactions to the pain, he must be desensitized to it. In some cases, the way to do this is to have him imagine, while deeply relaxed, that particular type of pain, first in a location remote from the chest, such as the lower abdomen, and then progressively closer to its site in the chest.

In other cases of agoraphobia, the person refuses to leave the house because he is afraid of certain kinds of people or objects he may encounter in the outside world—crazy people, automobiles, police, or tough-looking people who make him think of being mugged.

The most common kind of agoraphobia is found in unhappily married women who feel helpless and are unsure of themselves. They are low in "self-sufficiency"; that is, they find it difficult to fend for themselves. The fear of separation actually develops at the end of an intricate series of events in the woman's social and marital history. She has always been discouraged easily. She has never felt capable of making decisions on her own or of standing up to people. She may have married largely to have someone to lean on, a circumstance that would make a poor choice of partner quite likely. Over the years, she has become more and more disenchanted with the marriage, and efforts to improve it have failed. She has developed a growing impulse to get out of it, but she has taken no action. Her low self-sufficiency makes her afraid to withdraw from the shelter of her husband, even though she may loathe him. Frequently, she also dreads the condemnation of her parents, friends, or relatives that would arise if she were to break up a family. Nevertheless, she fantasizes about being free from the chains of her marriage. This enticing image unfortunately also arouses fears. As she indulges again and again in the fantasies, more and more fear becomes attached to them. And it becomes less and less possible for her to leave. When the fear becomes very great, it generalizes. It spreads from the image of being alone in a social sense to being alone in space.

Another and even more common way in which agoraphobia develops in such a woman is as follows. She is constantly in a state of high anxiety. One day, while driving a car, she has some dizziness or palpitations. These symptoms might make anybody somewhat anxious, but when that anxiety is added to the high level already present, the combination may amount to a state of panic. This panic is now associated with the circumstance of being away from home. The experience of being distant has thus become a trigger to panic. The panic reaction is automatic when she is far enough from home, and it may worsen with repetition. The distance at which she is comfortable may gradually lessen.

In one way or another, then, the fear of separation is the final link in a chain of emotionally potent events. To treat only the anxiety that results from the separation would leave the woman with her more basic fears. She *does* have a fear of separation, but the original network of fears must be treated if the secondary fear of space is to be lastingly eliminated. The original "weak" spot, the low self-sufficiency, is an anxious inability to cope with other people, including her husband. It is essential to overcome this. Assertiveness training is usually a vital ingredient in the therapy.

With agoraphobia, as with many other cases, it is obvious from the start that anxiety is the problem, and the main task of behavior analysis is to identify correctly the source of the anxiety. However, many people do not include anxiety among their complaints. Yet the behavior analysis almost invariably shows anxiety to be at the root. Common examples are sexual disabilities, stuttering, tension headaches, certain cases of asthma, and depression. (See "Fear in Disguise," in Chapter I.)

Let us take the example of stuttering. If a stutterer is asked whether he always stutters, he will almost certainly answer that he does not. His speech is likely to be flawless at home with his family; it is only in particular social circumstances, such as the presence of strangers, that he stutters. Further questioning brings out the details of the controlling factors. Does his stuttering get more severe if the other person is unfamiliar? Does it depend on the number of strangers present? Their age or sex? Their authority status? Their friendliness or hostility? There is always a relationship between the stutter and the amount of anxiety that a situation arouses: the more anxiety, the more severe the stutter. It follows that treatment that weakens the anxious response to strangers would diminish the stutter. This is exactly what happens. In many cases, no further therapy is needed; in others, however, a speech hesitancy that is unrelated to anxiety is also present and must be dealt with by vocal retraining procedures.

As we noted previously, while most neurotic fears are due to direct emotional conditioning, others are the result of some kind of erroneous belief. An important function of the behavior analysis is to determine in the individual case whether the fear stems from faulty thinking or whether it is a conditioned emotional habit.

Sometimes both a mistaken belief and an emotional conditioning contribute to the same fear, as the following case illustrates.

PEGGY, a 35-year-old accountant, noticed that some red pimples had broken out across her chest and shoulders. At first she thought little of them, but after a few days she chanced on a *Reader's Digest* article about a fatal skin disease called *lupus erythematosus*. She convinced herself that that was the cause of her pimples, and, after several weeks of self-inflicted terror, was referred to me by her physician.

Having heard her story, I sent her immediately to the medical school's leading dermatologist. His examination showed that her belief was absolutely unfounded. He explained to her with great care the actual cause of her pimples; he completely reassured her, and she was greatly relieved. But the pimples recurred from time to time. Whenever she saw them, she had some anxiety, even though she now *knew* that they were not harmful.

Logically, she should have felt no fear. So why was she still terrified by the red dots? The answer goes back to the ways in which fear habits are acquired, described in Chapter III. When a great amount of fear is aroused in relation to a certain thing, no matter what the reason, that thing tends to become hooked up with the fear. It will then have the power to cause fear. Peggy's wrong *idea* had first caused her to be afraid when she looked at the red dots. She was, then, in a state of fear *while she was seeing the dots.* Before the idea was disproved, this fear had become connected to the sight of the dots. They had acquired the power to evoke the fear automatically, without the idea. So Peggy's treatment required, first, dealing with her habit of thought, and then desensitizing the emotional habit that had been "born" of that idea.

Panic Disorder

As noted above, agoraphobia sometimes begins when a person has a panic attack away from home (for example, while driving a car); anxiety is conditioned to physical separation. The occurrence of a panic attack may also initiate a liability to further panic attacks, that is, "panic disorder." This has been the topic of a great deal of research during the past decade, but until recently the essential nature of the condition has remained obscure.

Recently, new light has been shed on the basis of panic attacks, largely through the work of Clark (1986)[2] in England and Ley (1985)[3] in this country. It is apparent that some individuals are predisposed to hyperventilate excessively when subjected to unusually prolonged anxiety. Such hyperventilation may generate strong physiological symptoms, such as shortness of breath, tachycardia, palpitations, and trembling, which trigger anxiety of uprecedented intensity, that is, panic. The panic subsides after a varying period, but meanwhile it has become linked to sensations resulting from hyperventilation itself. Even relatively low intensities of these sensations may become triggers to panic reactions.

This analysis leads to a systematic and effective plan of therapy (Wolpe and Rowan, 1988)[4] that does not include medication, but whose effects are lasting. After the usual behavior analysis has provided essential information about the case, the therapist has the patient hyperventilate—breathe deeply and rapidly, pausing only to report any symptoms that he notes. Usually, in the course of a minute or two, the patient will have reported a succession of sensations that he recognizes as precursors to panic. This experience is sufficient to convince the patient that overbreathing is the cause of the panic, and not some dreadful illness. The insight diminishes the patient's sense of helplessness, and it also provides a basis for showing him how to protect himself against hyperventilation—and thus against panic—by keeping his mouth firmly shut whenever he becomes aware of any ominous sensation.

This clears the way for the next therapeutic task, which is to overcome the maladaptive fears that were the cause of hyperventilation in the first place; and when this goal is achieved there generally will be no further need for control of breathing. In a considerable number of cases, however, the patient has become vulnerable to the possibility of panic attacks from rapid heartbeat or shortness of breath, however these are caused—even by exertion. It is then necessary to procure deconditioning of the anxiety response to these symptoms. This may be effected by systematic desensitization or by exposure to graduated inhalations of carbon dioxide (Wolpe, 1987),[5] which should only be attempted under expert medical supervision. The currently standard treatment of panic disorder with antidepressant drugs like imipramine only keeps the panic attacks in abeyance: they recur when treatment ceases. Its use should therefore be relegated to occasional cases in which the more fundamental measures described above are ineffective.

Depression

Depression is a very common affliction. It is also remarkable the amount of nonsense spoken and written about it. Quite often someone claims to have the answer to "the problem of depression." In fact, there is no single problem, and treatment depends on the basis of the depression.

There are three basic kinds of depression: "normal" or situational, endogenous, and neurotic. A person is depressed after he fails an exam and has to repeat a year of school, or at the death of a dear friend. He is less depressed by less important things, such as realizing that something he said has needlessly hurt another's feelings. These depressions are normal responses to events; they usually fade within hours, days, or weeks. A normal depression may, however, sometimes continue over a prolonged period; for example, if a family member has an extended illness or if there are persistent financial problems. Thus, some depressions that are severe or long-lasting are considered normal because they are justified by events in reality.

Endogenous (or biological) depression has a variety of causes. Prolonged cases are most often associated with manic-depressive illness, which may have both manic and depressive phases, or only the depressive phase. Other causes range from abnormalities of the menstrual cycle to the effects of certain drugs.

It is the third kind of depression, neurotic depression, for which behavior therapy is indicated, since it is based on useless fear. This kind of depression first emerged as a separate category when Kraepelin noted in 1913 that certain cases of depression displayed unusual emotional reactivity.[6] Although the diagnosis of neurotic depression was very widely accepted, it was very difficult to make it with assurance, because clear criteria were lacking. In time, a preference developed for the noncommittal appellation, "nonpsychotic depression."

New justification for "neurotic depression" emerged when Shagass et al. (1956) impressively demonstrated that neurotic depressions are characterized by high levels of anxiety, in contrast to low levels in endogenous depression.[7] His observations were corroborated by Perez-Reyes (1972)[8] and by other workers whose research has been summarized by Shagass (1981).[9] In parallel with these findings, I found many years ago that anxiety is the basis of cases of depression that lack the features that would mark them as endogenous (Wolpe, 1979,[10] 1986[11]). If neurotic anxiety is clearly present, it is helpful, but not indispensable, to establish that it is quantitatively related to the depression. Increases in anxiety are often associated with the worsening of depression.

The treatment is, as with other secondary effects of anxiety, determined by the findings of the behavior analysis. Depression has in practice been found to be related to anxiety in four contexts, of which two or more are often operative in the same patient. These contexts are: (1) as a consequence of severe anxiety that has been conditioned to a given situation, (2) as a consequence of severe anxiety based on erroneous cognitions, (3) in relation to anxiety-based interpersonal inadequacy, and (4) when a person is unable to shake off the effects of bereavement for many months or even years.

In a series of 25 cases of neurotic depression, treatment consisted of various combinations of anti-anxiety measures—systematic desensitization, cognitive correction, and assertiveness training—according to the makeup of the case.[12] The neurotic depression was overcome or markedly improved in 22 of the 25 cases. Two cases were unimproved, and one had repeated recurrences of depression, though at much lower levels than before. These three cases were also, in large degree, failures in terms of overcoming the anxiety. Nineteen of the 22 successful cases were followed up after at least six months and thereafter for an average of five years after treatment. None had relapsed.

In recent years, it has come to be widely accepted that cognitive therapy as described by Beck et al. (1985),[13] Rush and Watkins (1981),[14] and Shaw (1977),[15] has specific efficacy in the treatment of depression. In Beck et al.'s 1985 report, 67 percent of the cases were rated "recovered" or "much improved."[16] They assumed, however, that they were treating a homogeneous syndrome, an assumption that is flatly contradicted by the results of Akiskal et al.'s 1979 follow-up study of 100 cases of non-psychotic depression, of which 36 percent turned out to be endogenous in character.[17] To compare the effects of different agents on psychopathically mixed groups of depression is as futile as to compare the curative effects of pill A and pill B on a mixed group of patients, some of whom have tonsillitis and others pneumonia.

When Beck et al. reported success in 67 percent of cases of non-psychotic depression, they gave all the credit to cognitive therapy.[18] This was unjustified, because they had overlooked other sources of therapeutic change. It has long been known, as stated in Chapter X, that up to 50 percent of neurotic patients either recover or improve greatly with any form of psychotherapy; which is due to the fact that anxiety-incompatible emotions are often aroused in patients by the therapeutic interactions, and these can weaken classically conditioned anxieties. About half of the *neurotic* cases in Beck's population may be expected to have had their anxieties, and consequently their neurotic depressions, markedly ameliorated in this way. In addition, of the endogenous cases (which Beck did not distinguish), 27 percent would be expected to improve substantially in the course of a few weeks without treatment (Klerman and Cole, 1965[19]). To assess the real effect of cognitive therapy would require subtracting these other sources of improvement from Beck's recovery rate. In other words, cognitive therapy *per se* only accounts for a small proportion of the 67 percent of favorable results—and these would be expected to be the cases of depression related to cognitively based anxiety.

IX

Some Complex Cases

Complex cases are not at all exceptional; rather, they are the rule. Only occasionally, in clinical practice, does the simple fear that the individual initially describes—say, of heights—turn out to be all there is to the case. One never knows in advance that a problem is as clear-cut as it seems; that is why it is never justifiable to do without behavior analysis. Especially if the problem is severe, one is not likely to find the behavior analysis confirming exactly the picture that was first presented.

As information accumulates, the precise structure of a useless fear takes shape much as a sculpture emerges from amorphous stone. The treatment that is needed becomes correspondingly clearly defined. But sometimes unexpected information alters the course of therapy. This information does not necessarily come from the person's history; it may emerge from daily happenings between sessions.

This chapter describes in considerable detail the analysis and treatment of several complex cases, and some others more briefly. All of them illustrate how much more there may be to a problem than meets the eye, and to what a great extent the success of treatment depends, first, on the behavior analysis, and, second, on the ability of the therapist to carry out the required treatment.

A Case of Anxiety and Depression

ALICE, a 34-year-old divorced schoolteacher, complained of continuous anxiety, severe depressions, and the sense that she no longer was enjoying life. She generally felt hopeless. The story she told was that after she had had an anesthetic for an operation seven months earlier, she had several attacks of anxiety, accompanied by difficulty in breathing and hence the frightening thought that she would lose the power to breathe. Two months later, these attacks gave way to a continuous state of anxiety. She also had extreme fears of disease and death.

It was natural for her to feel that her emotional problems were due to the anesthetic, for several reasons. First, she had been terrified at the age of 2 when her tonsils were removed and she had bled severely. Second, when, at the age of 23, she had had her wisdom teeth extracted, she had fought the anesthetic in terror, lest she suffocate. She had been concerned about being able to breathe under a variety of circumstances ever since. For example, when swimming underwater she was always afraid that she might suffocate before she could get to the surface. Lastly, as we have seen, the attacks of anxiety that had begun seven months back were accompanied by some difficulty in breathing. There was thus a clear sequence of events, beginning when she was 2 and gathering momentum along the way, that led to her concern over losing her breath. But the story that emerged from my questioning was quite different.

About eleven months previously, after a depressing New Year's Eve party, Alice's unexciting date had dropped her at home. She experienced, in the empty house, a feeling of isolation that became terrifying as she was on the way upstairs to bed. She ran out of the house and drove to her parents' home, where the fear gradually subsided.

She had dismissed the incident when she had the operation in April. Close inquiry revealed that she had no fear either in anticipation of the anesthetic or afterward. She had been aware of no anxiety at the sight of the gas mask, the hissing of gas, the mask being placed on her face, nor of a feeling of being unable to breathe. Since she did not experience anxiety in relation to any of these things, it was highly unlikely that this anesthesia had significant emotional effect on her. Pointing to the same conclusion was the fact that a full week had passed between the operation and the first anxiety attack. By that time, she was already at home. She had not been anxious while recovering in the hospital—with its nurses, equipment, odors, and other related factors that might have become associated with a fearful anesthetic experience.

However, she had been profoundly aware of her aloneness in

the hospital. It reminded her of feelings years before, at the birth of her child, when the man who was then her husband was away on military service. She first felt anxiety when she was back at home a week after the operation. A Valium tablet she had taken in order to sleep made her feel detached and drowsy, intensifying the feeling of isolation; this led to a panic attack. The panic subsequently recurred whenever she felt drowsy after drinking liquor.

The feelings of isolation became stronger and virtually ever-present when a brief love affair in May came to a disappointing close. A week or two after this, the anxiety too began to be continuous. This happened because her sense of isolation had become continuous. Having no control over these feelings, she felt helpless and extremely vulnerable. At the same time, the constant anxiety inhibited the pleasant feelings that were formerly aroused in familiar situations. A vacation on a farm with a friend was no longer the happy occasion that it once had been; she no longer enjoyed traveling; she became frightened at the idea of taking care of her son. She concluded that she had suffered a mental breakdown, which made her still more fearful and brought her to the point of despair.

Further analysis revealed that Alice's problem was based primarily on interpersonal fears. She had always been a timid person who allowed others to impose on her. A lack of assertiveness had contributed to the failure of her marriage. Among other things, she had been unable to make reasonable requests of her husband and would go along with his wishes no matter how she felt. As she bottled up her feelings, she began to resent him and became sexually unresponsive. In contrast to their beautiful premarital sex life, she had never, during their six-year marriage, had a single orgasm. Her unassertiveness had more recently played a major part in maintaining her lonely way of life. Once she made a new acquaintance, she would reveal too much of herself too soon. In so doing, she would become very emotionally involved with someone she barely knew and then expect a similar emotional response in return. The result was that each possible new friend was turned off, and her loneliness became increasingly fearful as her efforts to remedy it failed time and time again.

Alice received twenty-five sessions of behavior therapy in the course of nine months. Using her day-to-day contacts with other people, I instructed her in appropriate assertiveness with members of her family and with people at work, and taught her how to treat suitors with restraint when attracted and to discourage them when not attracted. She was desensitized to being at home without a partner and being rejected by men, as well as to her frightening physical symptoms and her disturbing ideas of growing old alone and of dying. As these fear centers were overcome, her general depression and anxiety vanished. At the conclusion of treatment, she rated herself "95 percent cured." At a nine-month follow-up she had improved even further.

I successfully treated Alice's diffuse anxiety and inexplicable depression (sometimes called *existential neurosis*) by analyzing her emotional reactions into component constellations, and dealing with each of them by the appropriate technique.

A Fear of Marriage

Many people absolutely avoid marriage. Some do so as a matter of preference; others, because useless fear makes marriage impossible. Most commonly, there is a fear of involvement, of being tied down. Often, the fear has a claustrophobic quality; a fear of enclosement in elevators and small rooms is sometimes present, too.

> NORA, 33 years old, an attractive sociologist who had come to this country from Finland, had a different basis for her fear of marriage. Her work, social, and sex life had generally been satisfying. Several of her love affairs had endured for two or more years and were very intense in feeling, but almost invariably they were with men who did not want to get married.
>
> At first it seemed likely that, like most others who fear marriage, Nora was afraid of being tied down. But her childhood history provided grounds for a different explanation. Her father, who had worked in the postal service in Finland, was detached and uncommunicative. If his feelings were hurt, he would withdraw and refuse to talk to the "assailant" (usually his wife) for days on end. He was very quick-tempered and would become extremely angry at Nora for the smallest mistake or oversight. For errors in her homework, he would beat her fingertips with a ruler. He rejected any attempts she made to express affection or to communicate in any personal way — a compliment, an embrace, a gift, or a gesture of warmth. For many years she feared him; in adolescence she grew to despise him.
>
> Nora's mother was quite affectionate, but she was also a strong disciplinarian. She imposed rigid rules, and proclaimed that it was a child's duty to be warm and loving to her parents, no matter how the child really felt. Nora felt guilty if she opposed her mother in any way. Caught between her two parents, she developed a great fear of doing the wrong thing. She managed to do well in her studies, and at 19 she went to college to study sociology.
>
> Nora's erotic interests began to emerge only when she was in college. At 21, she had her first serious relationship, with Chris, a

young man with whom, after a prolonged friendship, she enjoyed a marvelous sex life. Within a year he proposed to her, and she was delighted to accept. Unfortunately, her parents demanded that the relationship be broken off when they discovered that she and Chris had spent a week together at a seaside hotel. Nevertheless, she continued to see him secretly for some months.

Chris was, she told me, the *one* person she might have married. He was eligible, he was the right age, and he offered the right combination of companionship, intelligence, and shared interests. After Chris, she always avoided anyone who was truly eligible. She did meet other men whom she felt she might marry, but instead of allowing those relationships to develop, she shied away from them. She felt comfortable enough to have a relationship with a man only if she found at least one of these requirements to be lacking—in other words, if she knew that she could never marry him. The reasons for this perplexing behavior, and precisely what there was about Chris that made marriage with him alone seem possible, came to light later.

Nora had several of these relationships in which marriage was out of the question. At 25, she developed a serious association with a man sixteen years her senior. He wanted to marry her, but when he saw that to her the age difference made marriage impossible, he resigned himself to the fact that they would never marry. Once he did this, she felt that the threat of marriage was lifted, and she greatly enjoyed sexual relations with him.

This affair was followed by one with a man who was her age and with whom sex was "excellent," but whose personality included some traits she found intolerable. He was obstinate in his political opinions, fastidiously neat, wanted her to serve him his meals at precisely the same time each day, and generally lived a life that was entirely too compartmentalized for her. He was followed by a "father" type—patient, affectionate, kind, and twenty-two years older than she—and a succession of other lovers, with each of whom she became sexually involved only when she and he both knew they could never marry. Still, she was often in love with these men and jealous when they were absent.

At the beginning of her fourth interview, Nora revealed the reason she could have formed a lasting association with her first love, Chris. She felt that there was nothing he could have done that would have made her want to break the bond. She felt no uncertainty about him; therefore, she had no fear. *Uncertainty was in some way implicated in her fear of involvement.* But why was she certain about Chris, yet uncertain about the other eligible men from whom she shied away?

I left this problem for the moment and gave further attention to Nora's social attitudes, including guilt, which had arisen originally from her parents' accusations and expectations. What emerged as central was that she was very uncomfortable about saying no. Partly to explore this, and partly as treatment, I set up role-playing at the end of the sixth session. I told her to refuse the request that I, in the role of a casual acquaintance, was about to make. I asked her if she would drive me from Philadelphia to Wilmington, a distance of about thirty miles. She politely refused. But doing so raised her anxiety level to 45! After five repetitions of the play-acting, the anxiety level came down to 20. Repeating this at the next session brought the anxiety level down from 15 to zero in three enactments. I then adopted the role of a woman whom Nora had met once, and asked Nora to lend me her new fur coat for the weekend, which she, on instruction, refused. Seven repetitions of refusing this presumptious request brought her anxiety level down from 50 to zero. During the next two sessions, the role-playing went on to deal with Nora refusing various unreasonable requests from people more and more close to her.

I decided to see whether or not my role-playing was more real than if Nora *imagined* herself in those situations, and found that the imagined situations were *more* realistic—because my participation in the role-playing was a source of distraction. I therefore decided to desensitize her by using imagined situations exclusively.

It then became clear from the examination of Nora's social difficulties that the obstacle to her forming permanent relationships was a *fear of disappointing someone*. The two problems—her social inadequacies and her avoidance of marriage—were really one problem. If she merely had to refuse a request to borrow a coat, the person would be only slightly disappointed, so Nora's anxiety would be relatively little. But this fear was minuscule in comparison to the terror she would feel if she disappointed someone in an important love relationship. If she met a man whom she could envisage as her life's partner, she would at the same time feel, "I really can't be certain; I might have to back out later. Then I'll be disappointing him . . . "

She had not had this fear with Chris because she knew him well when their intimacy began; she felt that she knew everything about him. This was not true of the others whom she thought of as eligible. These men always presented themselves from the outset as lovers. Since she did not know them very well, she was afraid that some trait might later emerge which would make her want to change her mind and back down from the marriage.

Having established this fear of disappointing someone as central to Nora's fear of "serious" involvements, I needed next, for purposes of desensitization, to know how the strength of this fear was related to various aspects of the relevant relationships. I found that the fear varied according to two factors: how deeply the man cared about Nora, and how long the relationship lasted. It was the latter that chiefly determined how strongly she felt committed to him, and, consequently, how much stress there would be in disappointing them. In carrying out the desensitization, I accordingly set up scenes in which a combination of these two factors would be present.

I began by using a fictitious man who was presumed to care very much for Nora, but whom she had known only for a very short time. I could then progressively increase the degree of commitment by increasing the number of times she had seen him. I started the desensitization by having her imagine, while deeply relaxed, that she was stating her intention of breaking relations with a man she had seen five times and with whom she had never slept. In the course of four presentations, her anxiety declined from 20 to zero. Then she imagined herself making this statement to a man who she had seen eight times and slept with twice. Anxiety came down to zero in seven presentations.

At the twelfth session, I continued to increase the duration of the relationship Nora was breaking, so that by the end of the session she was able comfortably to imagine saying, after an association of seven months, "It is not so pleasurable to me anymore." I intensified the poignancy of the scene by having the man say such sentimental things as "Why can't you remember all the beautiful, precious moments we've had together?"; to which she was prompted to respond, "There are no longer these beautiful moments." During the next four sessions, she was desensitized to other situations in which she might be "disappointing" people or acting contrary to their wishes. These included refusing invitations home from her parents, and requiring an official (such as a bank manager) to repeat several times an explanation she found unclear. We finally dealt with some rejection anxieties — for example, the anxiety aroused by not being recognized by an acquaintance whom she passed in the street. After sixteen sessions, all known areas of useless anxiety had been covered, and therapy was completed.

A year later, Nora reported being almost entirely free of her old useless anxieties and the resulting inhibitions. She had been having a very satisfying affair with a man she intended to marry after solving some financial problems. She no longer feared involvements that might lead to marriage.

A Multifaceted Case of Depression

Most people who come for treatment are in their twenties and thirties, so their recovery offers them the prospect of many years of emotional well-being. Other people are less fortunate. Their lives have already been largely ruined by neurotic suffering. This was the case with Christine, a graceful and intelligent woman of 56 who worked as a librarian.

CHRISTINE had deep depressions, which lasted for several weeks, once or twice every year. While depressed, she felt helpless and unable to carry out her daily activities. In recent years, she had had hundreds of migraine headaches. She had had over a thousand sessions of psychoanalysis.

In the behavior analysis, a number of fear centers emerged. We began with her early history. She was born in Chicago. She remembered her father, who had died when she was 6, as kind and gentle. He used to sing for her and tell her stories at bedtime. He gave her a special pillow, a "companion," which she always slept with and continued to do so until she married. He also protected her from her mother, who was sharp, mean, and brutal, beating her frequently with a strap for any number of reasons—the color of a dress, a dish not washed clean enough, an innocent remark made to a visitor about a family problem. Another form of punishment was being sent to her room alone for several hours. Her mother showed no affection or support, even when Christine arrived home with a good report card, or when she drew a picture "for Mommy." She remembered an incident when she forgot the address of a family friend and arrived at a boarding house by mistake. When she knocked at the door, a stranger opened it and invited her in. A group of people were having dinner around a large dining room table. They all stopped eating and looked at her. She was terrified and began crying when she realized that she didn't know them. She ran home. When she arrived, her mother scarcely bothered to listen to her and told her to stop crying.

She was a shy child and disliked her school years. With the few boys she dated in high school, she was scared of getting too sexually aroused because she thought she might lose control and "allow the boy to go too far."

After graduating from high school at 18, she became a writer for a fashion magazine in New York. It was there that she had her first sexual affair, which lasted for four months and which she enjoyed very much. At 22, she fell deeply in love with a married man who was separated from his wife. During the year that Christine and he lived together, they often had raging fights, followed by tearful reconciliations. But since his wife refused to grant him a divorce, Christine saw that the relationship could never be as she wanted it, and she broke it off. For several months afterward, she was depressed.

One night at a poetry reading she met the man who was to become her husband. Don was steady, quiet, patient, and quite attractive. A few months after the marriage she began to see that he was, in fact, too docile. He did not react to her; he did not get angry, nor did he express any strong affection. Their sex life was unsatisfying, since he consistently had premature ejaculations. They had two daughters, to whom he seemed as indifferent as he was to her. By this time, having given up her job and her freedom to commit herself to raising a family, she felt used and abandoned. Still, she tried to make the best of things, and waited nine years before divorcing him.

After the divorce, Christine began to notice her increasing anxiety. She could not get used to waking up alone; she missed her husband; and she had long since thrown away her companion pillow. The thought that one day both of her daughters would graduate from high school and leave home terrified her. She was alone in the house for three days one summer, for the first time in seventeen years, while her daughters were visiting their father. She felt continuously panicky, with a deep sense of loneliness and isolation, and was tremendously relieved when they returned.

The above information came out during the first two sessions. We then began to examine how her emotional problems were *currently* interfering with her life. She related a recent incident with her 16-year-old daughter, Cathy. She had reprimanded Cathy for not doing homework. Cathy told her to mind her own business. A few hours later she tried to give some advice about a boy whom Cathy had been seeing. Again her daughter rejected her advice. "I got the feeling," Christine said, "that she didn't want anything to do with me, that she didn't need me." I pursued this point: she was upset by any kind of rejection.

She then mentioned that she was soon to take a trip to California. The prospect frightened her, but she felt that it wouldn't be so bad "because my daughters are coming with me." This information confirmed two aspects of her fear of being alone: first, that she was afraid of being away from home, and second, that she feared the absence of her loved ones.

Relaxation training began at the fourth session in order to prepare her for desensitization. After daily practice for a couple of weeks, she was able to relax quickly and deeply. We began to work on the hierarchies for the two prominent fears that had emerged so far: aloneness and rejection. She had reported that she would not feel alone as long as she was *within sight of* someone she knew. If her daughter Cathy, for instance, was the only one at home and was to lock herself in her room — and therefore be out of Christine's sight — Christine would be very upset. In the desensitization, since we knew that she felt calmed by the sea, we began with images of a seaside cottage that she had visited. In the first scene, she imagined that she was in the cottage living room with Cathy, who was partly concealed by a bamboo screen. After two presentations, her anxiety level went down to zero.

I continued the desensitization by gradually altering two dimensions: I increased the distance her daughter was from her, and decreased her visibility. Christine imagined that Cathy was sitting in the next room with the door ajar, so that she was only partly visible. She later progressed to imagining Cathy out on the dunes, partly obscured by a white picket fence, at increasing distances.

At one of these sessions, Christine excitedly said that she had just realized what set off her depression. She had always known that she hated to be alone, but now she saw that it was precisely this feeling of loneliness, and the accompanying anxiety, that was the true cause of her depression.

We next turned to Christine's fear of rejection. In the desensitization, she first pictured a woman whom she had met and chatted with for a few minutes a week earlier. She imagined standing on the lawn at a garden party and seeing this woman look up at her. Christine waved to her and smiled, but the woman stared blankly at her and turned away. Again, two repetitions were sufficient to bring Christine's anxiety down to zero. Further scenes included: (1) Christine sitting at a café with a friend who excuses herself, gets up, takes her pocketbook, and leaves for a few minutes; (2) the friend excusing herself from the café and leaving for good from a luncheon date that they had scheduled weeks in advance; (3) Christine bumping into an acquaintance at the liquor store who is going to a party that Christine hasn't been invited to; (4) a friend in the guest room at the seaside cottage getting up and closing the door, thereby shutting Christine out for half an hour.

At one of the early sessions, Christine revealed that she also had a fear of flying. As the work on her fears of rejection and loneliness progressed, we began to deal with this other fear center. It had begun when she was a young woman and a friend of hers was killed in his own plane. Some years later her best friend's husband, who was a pilot in the air force, was also killed in a plane crash. Seven years after that, she saw through the mist at Nantucket a plane forced to crash-land in the water. The pilot was badly injured and screamed repeatedly for help; this had shaken her so badly that she was unable to walk. Her fear of airplanes had become so great that she was very tense if one passed far overhead, visible only for a second between clouds. She was jittery, although less so, when she noticed a plane on the ground; the closer the plane on the landing strip or in a field, the more anxious she became.

Because of the intensity of her fear, the first scene I had her imagine was a toy plane, with a wing span of four inches, that she saw in a shop window. Even this was a chilling scene for her, but it was more tolerable than the actual plane sitting in a valley a mile away. At subsequent presentations, the size of the plane was gradually increased, and a succession of larger and larger model planes was presented standing on a lawn; then she was gradually made to imagine boarding small private planes, at first silent and later with engines running. Eventually, an airliner at a museum was made a stepping-stone to the boarding of commercial airliners, which first made short flights and then transatlantic journeys. Once desensitized, Christine was able to fly wherever she wanted; she even came to enjoy the experience of flying in an airliner.

In a similar way, a number of other anxiety centers were identified and then overcome. These were (1) heights, (2) her mother (who was ill and who she sometimes had to visit), (3) waking in the morning, (4) her own early morning depressions (which made her anxious), (5) prospects of journeys, (6) being lied to, (7) urinating while someone was waiting outside, (8) saying good-by to loved ones (a separate fear from that of being alone).

After two years of treatment, at first twice and later once a week, Christine was much improved and no longer subject to anxiety—or depression—from any of the centers we had treated. When she telephoned me five years later to discuss a problem of one of her daughters, she said that she herself was still well.

Fear of Being Alone Based on Fear of Losing Control

In discussing agoraphobia in Chapter VIII, I drew attention to the fact that the true basis of this fear varies from case to case. Maria is an example of the commonly encountered case in which this fear arises from a dread of mental or physical illness.

MARIA was a 23-year-old single woman whose life was dominated by a fear of being alone. She needed someone with her to take charge because, as she believed, she might go out of her mind and lose control of herself. She would never consider walking away from her home unaccompanied, for then not only would she not have a companion to help her if the expected catastrophe were to happen, but she would not be able to summon help by phone.

Her fears were set off by an incident six years earlier, when she was a college freshman. While talking to a friend in her dorm at midnight, she began to feel blue at the thought that she was so fat that nobody would marry her. Suddenly, her hands sweated, her heart raced, and her head became numb. Thinking that something terrible was about to happen—that she would perhaps lose her mind—she was filled with terror. She rushed to the infirmary, where the nurse gave her a Valium tablet, which quickly put her to sleep. She awoke the next morning feeling fine.

About two weeks later, while shopping for a parka, she became depressed and demoralized on finding, after trying on fifteen or twenty of them, that none would fit. Driving home in this dejected state, she began to tremble uncontrollably and again felt the numbness in her head.

Terror of such severity surged up within her that she stopped at a garage and got an attendant to drive her home. From this time onward, she was never alone without fear.

Previous psychiatric treatments had been helpful only temporarily. Soon after the onset of her condition, a tranquilizer had made her considerably more comfortable, but after a few months it had lost its beneficial effect. A year before I saw her, a psychologist whom she had consulted, who claimed to know about behavior therapy, had suggested systematic desensitization, but he had not made a proper analysis of her case, and nothing had been accomplished.

At her second interview, I asked her what happened within her that made her think she might lose her mind. She said that being alone produced numbness, tension in the head, a sense of unreality, and a feeling of wobbliness when walking. She was convinced that a mental collapse would follow if these symptoms became any worse. As a first step, it was necessary to find the basis of the symptoms. Since it is well known that hyperventilation (overbreathing, which leads to *too much expulsion* of carbon dioxide from the blood) is a common cause of such symptoms, I asked Maria to sit back in her chair and breathe very deeply and rapidly. In the course of a minute, the following symptoms appeared in succession: dizziness, sweating of hands, rapid heart rate, numbness in the head, trembling, and a feeling of unreality. The more she hyperventilated, the stronger the symptoms were and the more fearful she became. As I pointed out to her, this proved that the dreaded symptoms were merely a result of her overbreathing without actually knowing it—for example, through frequent sighing. It was obvious that overbreathing, however marked, could not cause her to "lose her mind."

This discovery had two immediate therapeutic consequences. First, it removed her belief in an imminent danger; second, it enabled me to place at Maria's disposal a method for directly controlling hyperventilation and the unpleasant symptoms that were due to it. The method is very simple. I told her that it is practically impossible to hyperventilate through the nose, and, therefore, at the first sign of the onset of the symptoms, she should keep her mouth firmly shut. Maria was soon able to see for herself the effectiveness of this measure.

However, more needed to be done. Although Maria now fully understood the basis of her symptoms, the state of being alone had in the previous years become an autonomous trigger to fear, independently attached to being alone and increasing with the time and distance involved (see Chapter II). Maria was now put on a program of progressively longer journeys on her own. Before, she had not been able to attempt these excursions because of the fear of losing her mind, a fear she now saw to be groundless.

The result of a carefully planned program of exposures was that, in the course of two months, Maria was able to drive fearlessly alone all over Philadelphia, to take trips by air and eventually by train to her home three hundred miles away. About a month later, she took up employment in a city a hundred miles from her home, living alone in a rented apartment.

An Unusual Case of Male Sexual Failure

I mentioned in Chapter VI that the most frequent cause of sexual difficulties in men is anxiety about sexual performance itself. However, other sources of anxiety can have the same effect. I once reported a case of a young man who had been highly active sexually, in whom failure of erection began immediately after he had deflowered a virgin.[1] Great anxiety had been aroused in him because he had a fear of blood and injuries and he knew that he was injuring her. Desensitization to the injury fear situations was needed to overcome the sexual problem.

Here is another example of sexual failure due to anxiety that had nothing to do with the sexual situation as such.

TED, a very successful 44-year-old lawyer, stated, when I first saw him, that after many years of excellent sexual relations with his wife, Rhoda, he had had difficulty during the past two years in getting and maintaining an erection with her. At first I worked from the fact that on the occasion of the first appearance of this problem he had been unusually tired. Then, as frequently happens to others, he had begun to doubt his sexual capabilities, labeling himself "impotent." I therefore began with the gradual approach method described in Chapter VI, instructing him how to move toward intercourse in slow, unpressured steps. This strategy seemed at first to be helping, but after a few weeks it was evident that his sexual performance was quite erratic. He had, he said, "a nagging feeling of uncertainty" about his capacity to make love.

This impelled me to examine more closely his relationship with Rhoda. It emerged that she had for many years been subordinating her life to him. About four years before he came to see me, though, she had become dissatisfied with her situation and had consulted a therapist who encouraged her to be her own person instead of an appendage to Ted. After some months, she had begun in various ways to rebel. For example, she started to resist catering and playing hostess at the too frequent parties he insisted on throwing in order to make and consolidate professional contacts. Ted commented, "My feeling is that she has abandoned me." It was this feeling of rejection that interfered with his erotic responses and thus impaired his sexual function.

So after spending some time in establishing with Ted that Rhoda was entitled to her own life, just as he was, I encouraged him to discuss the relationship with her, to try to agree on what their rights and obligations should be. After a few weeks Ted was much better able to accept Rhoda's new role. The communication between them assured him that she had not abandoned him, that she still loved him. From her it removed the resentment that had caused her to behave in the ways that had made him feel she no longer cared. I also desensitized him during two sessions to some of Rhoda's independent acts. These measures soon resulted in the return of his sexual abilities, besides establishing a much improved general relationship.

A Many-Sided Phobia

Some cases are complex because a number of different factors affect one useless fear, and each must be taken into account in the treatment of that fear.

CHERYL, a 36-year-old English housewife, was afraid of being seen to vomit. She had no physical illness that might make her vomit, but the anxiety at the idea of being seen doing so made her feel nauseated when her stomach was full. She avoided social situations and public places. Because politeness and the social graces had been emphasized in her upbringing, she always felt it very important to behave well. Her fear had begun when she was 18 years old: At a Christmas party, after drinking heavily, she began feeling nauseated and became afraid that she might be seen vomiting. She had never actually vomited.

Several factors affected her fear of vomiting. The more recently she had finished a meal, the more nervous she felt about throwing up. Her fear was also affected by the number of people who were watching and how close they were. In desensitizing her, I first had her imagine that four hours after a meal one person was looking at her from a distance of a hundred yards. I then gradually increased the number of people, until she was eventually seen from that distance by thousands of people at a football stadium. Then, to bring the crowd closer, I had her imagine that she was standing on center court just before the championship match at Wimbledon.

At this point, I found other aspects of place to be important. Tennis at Wimbledon is played on a grass court. Cheryl said that grass was less anxiety-provoking than a hard surface. Having overcome her anxiety of the Wimbledon scene, we moved the imagined location to Forest Hills, site of the U.S. Open, where the courts are hard. Then it emerged that Cheryl's anxiety was increased if there was a roof over the place where she was being seen. We moved the tennis courts indoors. Another factor that affected her fear level was how difficult it would be for her to get away; if she felt confined, she was more anxious. We took this into account by introducing a locked gate with a time-delay switch that Cheryl could activate by pressing a button. At first, the gate would swing open only five seconds after she had pressed the button. But I gradually increased the delay, until Cheryl had to wait several minutes for it to open.

I now began to reduce the length of time since her last meal. Eventually, she could imagine without anxiety a scene that before would have been terrifying: standing on a concrete floor in front of a large crowd in an indoor sports arena, quite unable to get out, ten minutes after having eaten her most recent meal. At the end of her treatment, Cheryl was able comfortably to go to restaurants, movie theaters, shops, and any other public place that she had previously been forced to avoid.

Some Clinical Capsules

Baseless Jealousy

ADAM was a 28-year-old insurance salesman. His "suspicious nature" was threatening to wreck his engagement to Estelle. He would become fiercely jealous without any apparent reason. This jealousy had been responsible for the break-up of two other important relationships in the previous five years. The basis of his reaction was traced to certain things his father used to do. He had been a generous man who treated his family well, except on the frequent occasions when he was drunk; then he became touchy, jealous, and possessive. He would say, "You spent the afternoon in the kitchen with your mother; that means you don't like me." His jealousy was a kind of hurt anger, expressed in a tone that implied, "How can you do this to me?"

Adam now had the same kind of responses toward Estelle: when she behaved in any positive way to another man, or even spoke favorably about one, Adam felt that he had taken a back seat to that person. He felt the jealousy he had seen his father feel. Treatment consisted of desensitizing Adam to an extensive hierarchy of situations in which Estelle was praising, talking to, accepting rides from, and in other ways behaving in a friendly way toward men. As the anxiety was overcome, Adam lost his jealousy.

An Emotionally Caused Skin Disease

VERA was a 40-year-old elementary school teacher who, for the past five years, had been having severe attacks of a skin rash. The present attack had lasted for the past fourteen months; the skin around her face, neck, elbows, armpits, and thighs was inflamed and itchy. Her father had been a member of the foreign service, and she had been born in the Orient, the eldest of three children. She had gotten along well with her parents, but she hated the older of her two brothers both because he bullied her and because he often disregarded or insulted their parents. Vera would try to make up for his behavior by being especially affectionate or helpful. She had always detested anybody who caused those close to her to be miserable.

She recalled two exceedingly terrifying experiences. The first was when, at the age of 6, she came around a corner in Tokyo to see a Japanese adult masturbating with "an insane expression on his face." She had run away in terror and never mentioned the incident to her parents. Then, when she was 11, the family had spent a period of time on a volcanic island. She was in a state of terror during a tremor that went on for two weeks.

I made a list of everything she could think of that could possibly make her fearful or tense. I then divided these fears into three separate groups: (1) situations suggesting danger and misery, (2) being criticized or rebuked, and (3) failing to come up to expectations. We set up a program of desensitization that would eliminate the various gradations of anxiety associated with these situations. As we made progress in ridding her of her anxieties, the skin rash progressively diminished and eventually disappeared. There were only occasional and very mild recurrences when she was subjected to unusual stress.

The Spider Was Mother

JULIE, a 21-year-old psychology student at a Midwestern university, complained of a lifelong fear of spiders that had become especially bad during the past few months. At least once a week she had nightmares in which spiders were involved; for instance, they were thrown at her or surrounded her on a beach. Two years before, she had married and during the five unhappy months of the marriage her nightmares had ceased. On her return to her parents' house, they returned. It later became apparent that the spider fear and related nightmares were due to her mother's relentless grip on her life. The fear of spiders was finally eliminated when her fear of rebelling against her mother was overcome through a combination of assertiveness training and systematic desensitization.

In Julie's case, the fear of her mother—the true source of fear—had transferred to the image of spiders in her dreams. The spiders had, in a sense, become equated with her mother, as shown by the fact that the same feelings were aroused in Julie by the dream spiders and her real mother. This equation was later confirmed by the disappearance of the peripheral (symbolic) fear when the central one was eliminated.

The occasional occurrence of such symbolism does not justify dream

interpretation as it is commonly practiced. The creative assigning and interpretation of symbols, unless it is based on strong grounds provided by
the patient, is more appropriate to art and poetry than to psychiatry.

A Case of Fire-setting

OLIVER, aged 17, was sent for treatment by a probation officer because he had set two fires. The first, in an open field, had burned
nothing but grass. In the second, at the printing business where he
worked, he had ignited a large stack of blank paper by throwing
lighted matches from a balcony.

The behavior analysis revealed that before the first fire he had
been upset by a scolding from his father, and before the second he
had been berated by his foreman in front of his fellow workers for
arriving late to work. And there were other occasions when Oliver
felt humiliated and expressed his resentment in inappropriate ways.
For instance, when he was upset with his mother, instead of taking
her coat to the dry cleaner's as she had asked, he stopped along the
way and threw it into the river. He then returned home and told her
it had been stolen.

All these impulsive acts were due to his oversensitivity to dispar-
agement. Treatment consisted of systematic desensitization to unimportant criticism and disapproval, and of teaching him to resist the
pressures of rowdy friends to commit such acts as drinking while driving. This was essentially assertiveness training.

In fourteen sessions spread over three months, he overcame the
anxiety that had generated his inappropriate impulses. After four
years, there has been no further fire-setting or other antisocial behavior.

The cases described in this chapter were all convoluted in various ways.
The behavior analysis revealed in each of them a structure that was not
at all obvious at the initial presentation of the person's problem. Because
the descriptions are condensed from extensive interactions, they necessarily
omit many details, but they do provide a glimpse into the process of behavior analysis. The therapist must be sensitive to the words and feelings
of the patient while piecing together the interrelations between events in
the world and the patient's reactions to them.

The descriptions of the cases also provide some idea of the intricacies
of behavior therapy. Even when the behavior analysis yields a clear-cut
picture, the treatment that follows is not necessarily simple, and may not
move in a straight line.

The therapist must take many factors into account, and may switch
from one area to another and from one technique to another, according
to the feedback he receives.

X

Issues and Answers

Do All Therapies Work?

A multitude of therapies is available for emotional problems, including transactional analysis, primal scream, encounter group, nondirective therapy, psychodrama, EST, reality therapy, and the many varieties of psychoanalysis, among them Freudian, Jungian, Adlerian, Reichian, and Sullivanian. Each claims to be effective and superior to the others. But whenever therapies other than behavior therapy have been studied, they have all shown approximately the same level of favorable results: 40 to 50 percent recovered or much improved.

This percentage is enough to convince each therapist that his method is effective. And yet if the percentage of success is the same for all therapies, their results would seem to be due *not* to a particular procedure, but to something that is common to all of them. The one obvious common feature is the confidential interaction between therapist and patient. There is no doubt that in a great many patients feelings of hope, admiration, and respect are aroused by this interaction; and if anxiety-evoking matters are introduced—as when the person talks about what is bothering him—then it can be expected, because of the mutual inhibition principle, that *these emotions will inhibit any fear responses that are relatively weak*. In this way, the fear habits are weakened: the person improves. Similarly, reassuring explanations that the therapist comes up with may serve to calm the person who feels he has a grasp of something that previously was incomprehensible.

Meanwhile, the occurrence of these spontaneous emotional arousals during psychotherapy has been fortunate for untold numbers of people. It has benefited the patients of psychotherapists of many persuasions. The negative side of this is that therapists attribute their successes to their *methods* instead of to their own emotional impact, with the result that a good deal of time, effort, and money is spent on procedures that really do not help.

Unless it can be shown that a particular method or system yields a percentage of recoveries that is significantly greater than the 40 to 50 percent baseline, that method cannot be said to make any therapeutic contribution at all.

Is Behavior Therapy Better?

Does behavior therapy improve on the common run of results? The first published statistical analysis was of my own results. In an average of thirty sessions, 188 (89 percent) of 210 people I had treated were either apparently recovered or at least 80 percent improved. These judgments were based on criteria proposed by a distinguished psychoanalyst, Robert P. Knight: improvement in symptoms, increased productiveness at work, enhanced sexual function and enjoyment, better interpersonal relationships, and the ability to handle ordinary psychological conflicts and everyday stresses.[1] This impressive rate of improvement has since then been confirmed time and time again in clinical practice.

Alone among the systems of psychotherapy, behavior therapy yields a percentage of recoveries significantly above the baseline: 80 to 90 percent of patients are either apparently cured or much improved after an average of twenty-five to thirty sessions.

Further support comes from a large number of studies—two of which can be mentioned here—in which behavior therapy was compared to other treatments. In the first, conducted by Dr. Gordon L. Paul, psychoanalytically oriented therapists were asked to treat students who complained of fear of public speaking. (See the following section in this chapter.) They were, in each case, to employ one of three techniques: their own therapy, systematic desensitization, or a "placebo" procedure in which the student was given support and attention. After the treatment was carried out, the students (1) were asked how they now felt about public speaking, (2) spoke in front of a group of people, and (3) were physiologically monitored. All three of these indicators showed that the therapists did significantly better with systematic desensitization—even though they had only just been taught it in the simplest way—than with their own techniques or with the placebo procedure.[2]

In a second study, Dr. R. Bruce Sloane and his colleagues assigned neurotic patients to one of two treatments—behavior therapy or psychoanalytically oriented brief psychotherapy—or to a waiting list. After the four-month treatment period, the behavior therapy patients were the most improved on several measures. A one-year follow-up showed that only those who had been treated by behavior therapy maintained their improvement over those who had been put on the waiting list.[3]

Why Not Psychoanalysis?

For most of the twentieth century, hope for dealing with neuroses—useless fears and their consequences—has rested in psychoanalysis. Freud presented his theories in so extraordinarily beguiling a way that for three generations psychiatrists have believed neurotic sufferings to be the result of "repressed complexes." Memories of traumatic sexual experiences in early childhood are supposed to be imprisoned or repressed in what Freud called "the unconscious mind." He thought that this imprisonment was the mind's way of dealing with memories too painful to be allowed into consciousness. The neurotic symptoms were seen as expressions of emotional forces tied to these memories.

We need to distinguish between happenings of which we are unconscious and the unconscious mind. Obviously, our heartbeat, intestinal contractions, hormonal secretions, and so forth are unconscious. So are a great many of our movement responses—avoiding potholes on the road, lathering the soap when showering, flicking off the cigarette ash. These are examples from the vast repertoire of coordinated acts that we originally learned through conscious deliberation and that we now perform automatically. Coordinated automatic responses are indispensable components of the most complex skills. When a fine violinist plays a passage in a sonata, his conception of the music determines how he intends it to sound, but his performance depends on a broad array of automatic body and finger responses monitored by pressure, touch, and hearing. If he did not have these automatic responses at his disposal, and required conscious deliberation in the shaping of every note, the virtuoso feats to which we are accustomed would not be possible.

Another kind of unconsciousness or reduced consciousness is evident in our failure fully to experience many things that are present to our senses during the day—the subtle colors of a cloudy sky, the smells and sounds of a dinner that is being prepared, and so on.

We are also often unaware of our emotions and of their causes, including our useless fears: what really sets them off, when they began, how they are related to such other symptoms as depression. We may become increasingly tense during a work day without noticing the tension; we may have an uneasy feeling about someone, or be mysteriously attracted to him, though we do not know why. Take the example of the tension—it is there to be perceived; another person may notice the furrowed forehead or clenched jaws. But the fact that we are unaware of these things does not mean that we have an unconscious mind.

This point can be illustrated by examining a case that Freud regarded as demonstrating activity of the unconscious mind. A man who came to see him was deeply upset whenever the church bells rang in a village some distance from his home. This, it was later discovered, was because the sound of the bells was associated with a painful love affair he had had some years previously. The bells had become triggers to the man's emotional response, even though the upsetting situation was long past. Since the man did not immediately connect his distress with the love affair, Freud inferred that the connection between the two had been driven into the unconscious mind. But, as we have repeatedly noted in this book, an emotional response can be triggered by a particular occurrence because of previous conditioning. The sound of the bells had become a trigger to his distress, in much the same way as the setting sun was a trigger to the unhappiness of the man described in "What Can Be Feared," in Chapter I. To invoke an unconscious mind—an awareness within us that controls us and that we can never directly know—is unnecessary.

A cornerstone of psychoanalysis is the Oedipal theory: the young child being sexually attracted to the parent of the opposite sex. It is based on the tragic Greek myth of Oedipus, the son of a king, who unwittingly killed his father and then married his mother. When the facts became known, his mother hanged herself and Oedipus tore out his eyes. The tale is powerful and shocking, and Freud's assertion that it symbolizes the normal early emotional attitudes of sons to their parents had a stunning impact.

But the dramatic force of a theory has no relation to its truth. Direct observation of young children speaks against the Oedipal theory. For example, in England, C. W. Valentine examined the behavior of twenty-nine children from birth until the age of 8. He found that through the age of 4, a child prefers whichever parent does less punishing. After 4, the boys tend to prefer the father, because he is a better playmate. Whenever the parents put on a display of hugging one another, the reaction was almost universally positive—the children clapped their hands in pleasure.[4] All of this is contrary to the Oedipal theory.

Nor has psychoanalysis delivered the results it promised. The central goal of the treatment is to enable the supposedly repressed memories to surface. The main methods are free association and dream interpretation. In the former, the patient, lying on a couch, is encouraged to say whatever comes to mind. The idea is that if he can verbalize what he has repressed, he will release the attached pent-up emotions that are responsible for his symptoms. Once the emotional forces behind the symptoms are gone, the symptoms will disappear.

However, the statistical studies that have been carried out show that psychoanalytic treatment, even if it goes on for years, meets with no more success than other conventional methods, including the very simple kinds of treatment that people receive in general hospitals.[5] Particularly revealing was the 1958 report of the Fact-Gathering Committee of the American Psychoanalytic Association. About 50 percent of 595 patients who had undergone psychoanalysis were regarded as having been "completely analyzed." But *with respect to their symptoms,* only 60 percent of the completely analyzed patients (about 30 percent of the original 595) were judged cured or greatly improved. The results of a major study at the Menninger Clinic, reported in 1971, did not improve on the 1958 results.[6]

In recent years, there has been a movement away from formal psychoanalysis toward what is known as *psychoanalytically oriented therapy.* Instead of dream analysis and free association, the therapist tries to get at what is "unconscious" in a more direct way—by questioning the patient and by interpreting what he says. The emphasis is no longer on resolving Oedipal conflicts, but the task is still the uncovering of unconscious motivations. This therapy is vulnerable to the same criticisms as psychoanalysis and has not been shown to be any more successful.

Many people feel that even if psychoanalysis is not very effective, everyday life shows that its ideas are basically sound. If a man has an argument with his boss, he may come home and take it out on his wife. If an actor does badly at an audition, he puts the audition out of his mind. Superficially, these look like "unconscious processes." Actually, neither of them really demonstrates repression, because the experiences are easily available to be recalled.

The objections I have raised to psychoanalytic theory and practice do not detract from Freud's permanent contribution to psychotherapy. He was the first unequivocally to take the position that the causes of neuroses are to be found in the emotions and not in ideas. In a broader sense, he placed major emphasis on the nonrational, insisting that emotional forces compel us to do even ordinary things. Finally, he made the world confront the role of sexuality in human life and interactions. It is a lesser matter that he was mistaken in his detailed theorizings about these things.

In addition, it may be true that some of Freud's ideas which today seem tenuous (such as dream symbolism) will at some later date be found to cast valuable light on our mental and emotional life—if reliable relationships can be established. Dr. Paul L. Wachtel has advocated an interesting new use of psychoanalytically derived information. He believes that the kinds of experiences we have had in early life and our ways of dealing with them strongly influence how we perceive and deal with later experiences. Therefore, by revealing childhood patterns that have persisted into adulthood, we may increase the breadth of possible therapeutic change.[7] The practical value of this idea remains to be investigated.

Anger

Great emphasis has been placed by those who practice psychoanalytically oriented therapy on the role of anger in neurotic problems. They believe that many neuroses are the result of bottled-up anger and that the expression of that anger is what is needed to overcome the neurosis. The person needs to "get it out of his system." However, they see the expression of anger as something that should come spontaneously from the patient, rather than being suggested by the therapist.

This hands-off approach is typified by the following reported account. A psychoanalytically oriented therapist became aware that a woman patient of his was being stifled by her mother and that she needed to stand up for herself. The rules of his therapy, though, dictated that he should not tell her to express herself; instead, she was to arrive at that realization herself. This she eventually did—thirty sessions later. She then expressed her legitimate anger, and immediately began to improve.[8] A behavior therapist, by contrast, would have encouraged her to assert herself with her mother at a much earlier stage.

Very often, when people are continually angry with one another, what is required is not that they express this anger, but that the situation causing them to be angry be changed. This may seem self-evident, but the failure to recognize it is the basis of much misguided counseling. A husband and wife who are unhappily married may be angry with each other, each for legitimate reasons. The wife cannot stand the fact, for instance, that her husband brings people home to dinner without calling her, or that he often comes home late from work. The husband may be angry with her for insufficiently disciplining the children. Resentment builds on both sides. A therapist or marriage counselor schooled in the "let out your anger" philosophy would probably encourage them to spend their sessions with him expressing their bottled-up anger. But this strategy would accomplish very little, since the grounds for the anger remain. In fact, an excellent series of studies has shown that people who express their anger *merely become angrier* than those who are patient in a trying situation.[9]

A more effective approach would be for the therapist to find out what each partner wants of the other and to arrange a "contract," whereby each gives the other what he or she asks, within reason. This strategy was developed by Dr. Richard B. Stuart.[10] Through the mediation of the therapist, the husband undertakes to let his wife know if he will be late from work, and she undertakes to pay attention to disciplining the children. Other requests are similarly taken into account and included in the contract. The aim is for both to be satisfied and the grounds for anger removed. Many marriages have been saved by this strategy.

Anger that comes to the attention of psychiatrists is usually the result of unexpressed resentment. But the situation in which the anger is expressed may be completely different from that in which the resentment built up.

In other words, the person lets off steam, or takes out the anger on some-one else. Such expression is misplaced and has no effect on whatever caused the resentment. *Anxiety is what usually prevents the expression of resent-ment at the appropriate time.* Thus, indirectly, the real root of the anger is anxiety. What is needed to solve the problem is *not* the venting of anger, it is the elimination of the anxiety. This is illustrated, with a twist, in the case of Gene.

> GENE, a 58-year-old retired journalist, came to see me because his wife was fed up with his surliness and extreme irritability. She told him that she could not continue in the marriage unless he changed his personality. Gene had retired after having a heart attack; he was now writing a novel at home and had taken charge of the household work. He made breakfast, for instance, for the family. If his wife disrupted his breakfast plans by telling him at the last minute to use the pancake batter that she had put away the night before, he flew into a rage. Or his temper was set off when she asked him at night to check that the front door was locked. Since he wanted to stay mar-ried to her, he was very eager to overcome his irritability.
>
> It seemed to me that he should have been able to tolerate such annoyances without flying off the handle, so I set about desensitizing him to these situations. (Desensitization can be used to diminish anger reactions as well as anxiety.) We succeeded in greatly reducing the amount of anger he felt in response to these day-to-day situations, but he was still resentful about them.
>
> One day Gene came in feeling extremely upset. I asked him why. The reason, he said, was that he had given in to his wife's wishes to move to an apartment in the city, even though he had no desire to do so. It then unfolded that this submissive behavior had been go-ing on for the entire fourteen-year marriage. He was so afraid of los-ing his wife that he constantly gave in to her. Instead of expressing his annoyance when she insisted on having her own way, he was endlessly accommodating—but he always resented her taking advan-tage of him. I then set about training Gene in assertiveness so that he could stand up for what he wanted. Since his wife would not ac-cept that, she left him soon afterward. But instead of being upset, they were both greatly relieved, for they had come to realize how in-compatible they really were. Gene later developed a satisfying rela-tionship with another woman.

In this case, the central problem was not the anger overreaction, but the husband's lack of assertiveness. That was the "twist": even though the desensitization was working, and his temper was being toned down, assertiveness training was what was really required to remove the source of his anger. In other cases, though, the anger overreaction is central, and desensitization can be used to overcome it.

"Exposure" — A Word Posing as a Theory

Behavior therapy has often been burdened by "concepts" that have no relation to established knowledge of the learning process, but have nevertheless been used to throw doubt on accepted behavioral practices or the principles on which they rest. The most recent and popular of these concepts is the theory that the true basis of overcoming maladaptive anxieties is not reciprocal inhibition or the like, but "exposure." This theory has been particularly vigorously promoted by Marks (1975, 1981[11]) and Agras (1985[12]). They argue that the solitary factor common to all procedures that bring about the weakening and extinction of maladaptive fears is exposing the patient to fear stimuli. The indispensability of exposure is incontestable, but also banal; exposure to the stimulus is *always* involved in both the process of connecting a stimulus to a response (learning) and the process of disconnecting it (unlearning). The question to be answered is: What events must co-occur with exposure to bring about learning on the one hand and unlearning on the other?

At an early stage in this book, some known determinants of learning and unlearning were discussed. The proponents of exposure propose nothing at all. Marks says that the patient "gets used" to the stimulus, but this is just another way of saying that fear decreases.

In the ordinary course of the patient's life, repeated exposure to anxiety-evoking stimuli has not weakened the anxiety. It *could* be weakened by various procedures, such as systematic desensitization, whose basis in response competition has been supported by numerous studies. Marks and Agras have disputed this on the basis of their own experiments, but these are in various ways flawed. For example, Benjamin, Marks, and Huson (1972)[13] found no difference between desensitization with and without relaxation, but their relaxation patients had received only one session of relaxation training from a psychiatric resident who had himself had only one session of training. Borkovec and Sides, in a survey of therapeutic studies noted in 1979, found that for relaxation to make a difference requires at least four training sessions. Without relaxation training, the emotional response to the therapist can provide response competition.[14]

It is noteworthy that Agras, after a string of experiments that led him to reject other mechanisms of fear reduction, *logically* reached the conclusion that the only thing that works is exposure.[15] Yet he acknowledges that of his patients so treated "few had fully recovered." This being so, "exposure" therapy can scarcely be called an advance in comparison with the 88 patients treated by reciprocal inhibition (Wolpe 1958[16]), of whom 28 *were apparently cured,* and another 50 much improved.

It is important to realize that in the foregoing comparison between therapy based on reciprocal inhibition and therapy based on what purports to be exposure is misleading because the exposure does not really occur in isolation. Whenever, under any circumstances exposure to a stimulus is followed by weakening of a fear response, *something else must been happening at that time,* this remaining true whether or not the proponents of exposure are indifferent to its accompaniments.

Personality and Change

In line with the criticism that behavior therapy is only for problems that are "on the surface" is the idea that it does not change personality. But what is personality? It is usually not defined, yet most of us have some idea of what the word means. If we say that someone has a sense of humor or is shy or is loud and obnoxious, we are really referring to certain habits that we see in him. Most of what we usually think of as "personality" may be described as the sum total of an individual's habits. A man's personality is shown in what he does, how he behaves, what upsets him, what he wears and thinks, and how he deals with others. Is he sullen when he wakes up in the morning? Does he wear flashy clothes? Perhaps he thinks of himself as above the women in his life, or he regards them as his equals, or he is dominated by them. Is he excited by watching football games? Is he interested in nature? Does he go to church? Does he believe in God? Would he accept a bribe? Is he financially capable? Is he kind or ruthless? Does he like to be touched? Is he capable of repairing things that break around the house? Does he like children? Does he enjoy art, music? What kinds—classical, rock, jazz? Is he politically aware? What are his political leanings? Does he spell out his goals in life? What are those goals? Does he have a sense of humor? What kind of sense of humor? Is he witty or charming, or does he just like to laugh when other people are funny? Is his humor sarcastic or slapstick?

There is no doubt that when an individual is able to overcome his fears and other disabilities, he feels different: he has an enhanced self-image and an increased feeling of strength and freedom. He acts differently, feels different, thinks of himself in a new light. All of these are personality changes—new habits that are the consequence of removal of those fears and their progeny.

Personality change is thus a matter of habit change (through learning). Anxiety habits and other emotional habits form only a part—albeit a tremendously important part—of a larger framework. The many other habits that make up personality may also be changed by a creative application of the behavioral principles of reinforcement, extinction, and response competition. B. F. Skinner has shown how reinforcement principles can be used to enable people to develop behavior patterns to their own advantage.[17] Another notable development is James G. Taylor's account of the development of perception.[18] He ingeniously explains how a child learns to recognize distinct objects from the thousands of jumbled images that he takes in through his eyes.

Some Mistaken Notions

One of the commonest misconceptions about behavior therapy is that it can deal successfully with "surface" problems, but does not get to the "deep-seated" basis of neuroses. It treats "symptoms" but not "causes." This criticism, which has come to be widely accepted, stems directly from the psychoanalytic theory that something else lies beneath every problem. It conceives of neurotic symptoms as discharges of pent-up forces. If one symptom is removed, another will pop up in its place. In other words, either "symptom substitution" or relapse should occur. In fact, the effects of behavior therapy are lasting and profound; symptom substitution and relapse hardly ever occur. If they do, it is because of incomplete treatment: the therapist may have overlooked something, or the patient may have left treatment before it was finished.

Another misconception is that behavior therapy is applicable only to simple, limited, and well-defined problems, such as phobias, but not to complex cases. But as we have seen in the numerous examples in this book, it is applicable to the entire range of neurotic problems.

It is sometimes said that behavior therapy is cold and mechanistic, disregarding a person's feelings and thoughts. There may be several reasons for this notion. One is the language of behavior therapy, which, since it originated in experimental science, has tended to retain a technical tone. A second is that behavior therapy has repeatedly been represented in the press, incorrectly, as made up of cruel and degrading treatments that emphasize aversive shocks and include sensory deprivation, brainwashing, electroconvulsive therapy, and psychosurgery. A particularly baneful influence in this direction was the film *A Clockwork Orange*, in which a repulsive and entirely fictional treatment was seen as behavior therapy.

Cognitive Therapy

Recent years have seen the emergence of the viewpoint that *all* maladaptive fears are due to cognitive errors or distortions (Beck, 1976[19]; Ellis, 1974[20]; Mahoney, 1977[21]; Meichenbaum, 1975[22]). Essentially, they suppose that some kind of idea of danger is the universal mediator of fear. If neurotic problems were all due to wrong ways of thinking, then thought correction *would* always be what is needed to overcome them. While the cognitivists unflinchingly assert that this is the case, it should be noted that in practice they frequently use behavioral procedures such as assertiveness training and systematic desensitization, which they view as part of cognitive therapy! (e.g., Beck[23]). This is somewhat like a pitcher insisting that the game of baseball consists solely of pitching. When someone brings up the fact that hitting and fielding are also involved, he replies,

"Well, pitchers also field and hit. So these other activities are really only a sub-group of pitching." But pitching is included in baseball just as cognitively based fears are included among other maladaptive habits.

Many facts contradict the view that all fears are cognitively based. When a situation that is encountered in reality evokes anxiety, seeing it pictured or imagining it also usually evokes anxiety (Wade, Malloy, and Proctor, 1977[24]), though the subject can scarcely be *believing* that the image is dangerous. He simply responds to it with anxiety. Most neurotic patients know that the situations they fear are not dangerous, and contrary to Beck's view,[25] their knowledge is unshaken while actually feeling fear. A person with a fear of dead animals may be anxious when he sees one a hundred feet away, even though it is not dangerous and he does not regard it as so.

The cognitivists appear to be misled by the fact that cognitive operations are involved in deconditioning procedures like desensitization — as indeed they are in most human interactions. While cognitions of the patient and the therapist are inevitably involved in the desensitization procedure, the effect of the procedure is to diminish small measures of conditioned anxiety. The patient perceives the fact of change *secondarily, after the event.* This is quite different from the correction of thinking that is primary in the treatment of a cognitively based fear.

The fact that not all fears are based on wrong beliefs also emerges from the following two contrasting scenarios.

In the first, a man pointing a gun at me makes me fearful, with good reason — I perceive danger in the situation. A picture of a man pointing a gun at me does not make me afraid. In the real situation, I *believe* (rightly) that there is danger (I know that guns can kill people, that he is capable of pulling the trigger, etc.). When I am merely looking at a photograph, however, I *believe* (again rightly) that there is no danger. And I feel no fear. Therefore my fear is based on belief.

In the second scenario, a man sees a spider and feels fear. In clinical practice, it is usually found that an image (imagined or real) of a fearful object also produces fear, to a varied but often considerable degree. This man now sees a picture of a spider and he still feels fear. He does not believe that the picture of the spider can actually hurt him: there is *no* danger here, yet he still feels fear. The explanation cannot be based on a belief in danger, since if that were its basis, there would, as in the case of the gun, be no fear of the picture. Thus, the fear must be an automatic emotional response to the spider.

Meanwhile, the cognitivists have done a remarkable propaganda job in spreading the belief that their views of neuroses and psychotherapy constitutes a "revolution" in the field. So successful has this propaganda been that, in the minds of many, the cognitivists' position is seen as a modern advance on behavior therapy. The weaknesses of this viewpoint have been indicated above. Another consideration is that if cognitivism had been an advance, the addition of the ideosyncratic procedures advocated by therapists like Ellis and Beck would have improved on the outcomes achieved by standard behavior therapy. Latimer and Sweet (1984) in a review of studies relevant to this point, found no evidence that superior outcomes result from the addition of the methods.[26] A number of other studies (e.g., Biran and Wilson, 1980[27]; Emmelkamp and Mersch, 1982[28]) point to the same conclusion.

The Limits of Behavior Therapy

Since behavior therapy consists of procedures that bring about learning, it can be applied appropriately only to conditions that have come about through learning. One cannot expect behavior therapy to be useful for conditions that are not based on learning—for example, those due to biological illness of the nervous system. Thus, it has no value as a cure for schizophrenia, for which growing evidence of a biological basis has accumulated in recent years. However, in certain cases of schizophrenia, there is a predisposition for the person to *learn* certain bizarre habits, and these can be successfully treated through the use of learning principles. But it must be emphasized that this is a very limited accomplishment and does not amount to a cure of the illness.

Similarly, behavior therapy is of no use for treating other psychoses, such as manic-depressive illness, or other kinds of biologically based depression. In discussing depression in Chapter VIII, I drew attention to the usually overlooked fact that many depressions are just a normal response to loss or failure. Since the reaction is normal, there is no need for habit change; therefore, behavior therapy is not called for. What is called for is the support, comfort, and understanding of friends, and occasionally the temporary use of medication.

In many instances, the mere passage of time is all that is needed to end the depression—allowing the impact of the causative experience to fade. In other cases, some change in the person's life circumstances is required, and this is where a therapist may be helpful. For example, a deeply depressed young man once consulted me because he could not bear the medical studies to which he had already devoted almost two years. I discovered that his real preference was for law, which he had originally rejected because it was not "socially useful." I convinced him that all occupations have social value. He switched to law, lost his depression, and eventually became a distinguished lawyer. Similarly, a 30-year-old married woman came for treatment of depression that turned out to be caused by the unreasonable stranglehold her husband imposed upon her activities. The answer lay in changing his behavior, not in her having therapy.

Prevention and Extension

One of the most important values of behavior therapy that has, as yet, been little recognized is its use as a preventive means. Since we know how common fears are produced and how to treat them, it should also be possible to devise preventive programs. Several studies have indicated that a kind of "vaccination" can work. Consider a situation in which useless fears commonly develop, such as public speaking. It has been shown that people who are desensitized to speaking in public *before* they develop the fear of doing so become more resistant to that fear.[29] The same preventive use may be applied to fears of flying, criticism, being alone, rejection, and so on, thus obviating the depressions, stuttering, and other conditions that might result from those fears. The desensitization could be carried out when the person is young, as protection against anxiety — a kind of "preschooling in courage."

A second preventive measure against useless fears is educating parents not to punish their children in needlessly stressful ways. For example, if a child who is already afraid of being alone is locked in his room, he may develop a strong fear of aloneness or of enclosed space. Similarly, as we have seen, fears of masturbation or of sex may be started if a child is indoctrinated with the idea that it is sinful or dangerous. The serious harm that parents can unintentionally inflict is illustrated by the case of a young man whose younger sister was afraid of being alone. To comfort her, the parents had made him share a bed with her until he was 16. He began having sexual feelings toward her and felt guilty about them. Later, he became angry with his parents for having exposed him to this incestuous sexual excitement, and then felt guilty about his anger. He came to regard himself as an unworthy and despicable person, which, after a time, led to the idea that contaminating anyone with his urine would be reprehensible. He spent most of his waking hours in elaborate rituals of bathing, washing his hands, and cleaning his private parts. Parents should be awakened to such emotional hazards to which they may unwittingly expose their children.

Another extension of behavior therapy might be the changing of subtle personality traits that are not ordinarily thought of as requiring therapy. We may take as an example the story related to me by a young man. One evening he was walking along a riverbank with a young woman whom he had recently met. The girl stopped and sat on the low brick wall that lined the quay. He found her attractive. It was a warm night, and he could smell her light perfume. He felt that he wanted to hold her hand, to touch her. He did so. She responded, and they continued chatting. Then he wanted to brush her leg. He did so, lightly. But then, as he tried to kiss her, she turned away. The evening continued, and the conversation continued, but the young man felt hurt: he was disappointed by what he had not gotten.

He felt weepy, unloved, lonely. Later, while walking home alone, he began to think about what had happened. He realized that he had not been satisfied with the pleasure of being with her, or the beautiful evening and the river, and that he had found himself making sexual advances even though he hardly knew the girl. With all the possibilities of the wonderful evening there to be enjoyed, he mused, he had ended up getting upset because he could not have everything at once. Now, having come to these realizations and having taken the further step of deciding that he wanted to change his attitudes and behavior, how would he go about it?

It is not the kind of problem for which a person is likely to think of going to a therapist. I chanced to hear this young man's story in a context outside my professional practice. The most probable cause of his difficulty was that he had an undue sensitivity to rejection in certain situations. If he were desensitized to this, he would become less "at sea" in his relationships with women, better able to control the pace of relationships. Anxiety was a kind of boundary around certain aspects of his personality, cordoning off some areas from growth or change.

If people could become more aware of the effects of anxiety in their lives, they might seek treatment for such subtle problems. These could, as a rule, be overcome with very little effort, preventing in some cases the development of more serious emotional problems. Thus, a future goal is to increase people's awareness of these problems and their effects, and of the help that is available.

Behavior therapy consists of the practical use of experimentally derived knowledge of learning. Yet up to now, only a very small amount of the available knowledge has been used to solve human problems. Future developments should tap this already rich source, as well as expand it through laboratory research expressly designed to uncover new clinical methods.

Notes

Chapter I

1. A. Wohlgemuth, *A Critical Examination of Psychoanalysis* (London: Allen and Unwin), 1923; C. W. Valentine, *The Psychology of Early Childhood*, third edition (London: Methuen), 1946.
2. It is an interesting fact that the pain itself does not come to be arousable by the surrounding stimuli.

Chapter II

1. J. B. Watson and R. Rayner, "Conditioned Emotional Reactions," *Journal of Experimental Psychology*, 3:1, 1920.

Chapter III

1. L. Wittgenstein, *Philosophical Investigations*, third edition (New York: Macmillan), 1968.
2. R. W. Brown, *Words and Things* (Glencoe: Fress Press), 1958.
3. C. S. Sherrington, *The Integrative Action of the Nervous System* (New Haven: Yale University Press), 1906.
4. E. Gellhorn, *Principles of Autonomic-Somatic Integrations* (Minneapolis: University of Minnesota Press), 1967.
5. J. Olds, "Mapping the Mind onto the Brain," in *The Neurosciences: Paths of Discovery*, F. G. Worden, J. P. Swazey, and G. Adelman, eds. (Cambridge: Colonial Press), 1975.
6. From "The Great Lover," in *The Collected Poems of Rupert Brooke* (New York: Dodd, Mead), 1948.
7. A. Amsel, "Frustrative Nonreward in Partial Reinforcement and Discrimination Learning: Some Recent History and a Theoretical Extension," *Psychological Review*, 69:306–328, 1962.
8. J. G. Jenkins and K. M. Dallenbach, "Obliviscence during Sleep and Waking," *American Journal of Psychology*, 35:605–612, 1924.
9. D. Phillips with R. Judd, *How To Fall out of Love* (Boston: Houghton Mifflin), 1978.

Chapter IV

1. I. P. Pavlov, *Conditioned Reflexes*, trans. by G. V. Anrep (New York: Liveright), 1927.
2. Ibid.
3. Summarized in J. Wolpe, *Psychotherapy by Reciprocal Inhibition* (Stanford: Stanford University Press), 1958, Chapter 4.

4. J. H. Masserman, *Behavior and Neurosis* (Chicago: University of Chicago Press), 1943.
5. E. Jacobson, *Progressive Relaxation* (Chicago: University of Chicago Press), 1938.

Chapter V

1. Watson and Rayner, "Conditioned Emotional Reactions," 3:1–14.
2. M. C. Jones, "A Laboratory Study of Fear," *Journal of Genetic Psychology,* 31:308–315, 1924.
3. D. R. Stone, "Responses to Imagined Auditory Stimuli as Compared to Recorded Sounds," *Journal of Consulting Psychology,* 19:254, 1955.
4. Ibid.
5. J. Wolpe, *The Practice of Behavior Therapy* (New York: Pergamon Press), 1973, pp. 146 et seq.
6. Ibid., pp. 182 et seq.
7. E. Jacobson, *You Must Relax* (New York: McGraw-Hill), 1962.
8. Such a program is currently available at the Behavior Therapy Unit in the Department of Psychiatry, Temple University Medical Center.

Chapter VI

1. Assertiveness training was first extensively employed by Andrew Salter. (See his *Conditioned Reflex Therapy* [New York: Creative Age Press], 1949.) However, he saw it as "excitation," not realizing that its therapeutic effect is to weaken fear habits.
2. R. E. Alberti and M. L. Emmons, *Your Perfect Right* (San Luis Obispo, CA: IMPACT), 1978.
3. H. Fensterheim and J. Baer, *Don't Say Yes When You Want to Say No* (New York: Dell Publishing), 1975.
4. See R. B. Stuart, "Operant-Interpersonal Treatment for Marital Discord," *Journal of Consulting and Clinical Psychology,* 33:675–682, 1969.

Chapter VII

1. N. Malleson, "Panic and Phobia," *Lancet,* 1:225, 1959.

Chapter VIII

1. R. R. Willoughby, "Norms for the Clark-Thurstone Inventory," *Journal of Social Psychology,* 5:91, 1934; see also J. Wolpe, *Practice of Behavior Therapy,* p. 279.
2. D. M. Clark, "A Cognitive Approach to Panic," *Behavior Research and Therapy,* 24:464–470, 1986.
3. R. Ley, "Agoraphobia, the Panic Attack, and the Hyperventilation Syndrome," *Behavior Research and Therapy,* 23:79–81, 1985.
4. Wolpe J. and Rowan V. C., "Panic Disorder: A Product of Classical Conditioning," *Behavior Research and Therapy,* 1988. (in press)

5. J. Wolpe, "Carbon Dioxide Inhalation Treatments of Neurotic Anxiety," *Journal of Nervous and Mental Disease,* 3:129–133, 1987.

6. D. Kraepelin, *Lehrbuch der Psychiatrie,* eighth edition (Leipzig: Barth), 1913.

7. C. Shagass, J. Naiman, and J. Mihalik, "An Objective Test which Differentiates between Neurotic and Psychotic Depression," *Archives of Neurology and Psychiatry,* 75:461–471, 1956.

8. M. Perez-Reyes, "Differences in Sedative Susceptibility between Types of Depression: Clinical and Neurophysiological Significance," *Recent Advances in the Psychobiology of the Depressive Illnesses,* T. A. Williams, M. M. Katy, and J. A. Shields, eds. (Washington: Government Printing Office), pp. 119–130, 1972.

9. C. Shagass, "Neurophysiological Evidence for Different Types of Depression," *Journal of Behavior Therapy and Experimental Psychology,* 12:99–111, 1981.

10. J. Wolpe, "The Experimental Model and Treatment of Neurotic Depression," *Behavior Research and Therapy,* 17:555–565, 1979.

11. _____ "The Positive Diagnosis of Neurotic Depression as an Etiological Category," *Comprehensive Psychiatry,* 5:449–460, 1986.

12. _____ "The Experimental Model and Treatment of Neurotic Depression," *Behavior Research and Therapy,* 1979.

13. A. T. Beck, S. D. Hollon, J. E. Young, and R. C. Bedrosian, "Treatment of Depression with Cognitive Therapy and Amitriptyline," *Archives of General Psychiatry,* 42:142–148, 1985.

14. A. J. Rush and J. T. Watkins, "Group versus Individual Cognitive Therapy: A Pilot Study," *Cognitive Therapy and Research,* 5:95–103, 1981.

15. B. F. Shaw, "Comparison of Cognitive Therapy and Behavior Therapy in the Treatment of Depression," *Journal of Consulting and Clinical Psychology,* 45:543–551, 1977.

16. Beck et al., op. cit.

17. H. S. Akiskal, R. H. Rosenthal, T. L. Rosenthal, et al, "Differentiation of Primary Affective Illness from Situational, Symptomatic and Secondary Depression," *Archives of General Psychiatry,* 36:635–643, 1979.

18. Beck et al., op. cit.

19. G. L. Klerman and J. O. Cole, "Clinical Pharmacology of Imipramine and Related Antidepressant Compounds," *Pharmacological Review,* 17:101–141, 1965.

Chapter IX

1. J. Wolpe, *Psychotherapy by Reciprocal Inhibition,* pp. 152 et seq.

Chapter X

1. R. P. Knight, "Evaluation of the Results of Psychoanalytic Therapy," *American Journal of Psychiatry,* 98:434–441, 1941.
2. G. L. Paul, *Insight Versus Desensitization in Psychotherapy* (Stanford: Stanford University Press), 1966.
3. R. B. Sloane, F. R. Staples, A. H. Cristol, N. J. Yorkston, and K. Whipple, *Psychotherapy Versus Behavior Therapy* (Cambridge: Harvard University Press), 1975.
4. C. W. Valentine, *The Psychology of Early Childhood.*
5. D. M. Hamilton and J. H. Wall, "Hospital Treatment of Patients with Psychoneurotic Disorders," *American Journal of Psychiatry,* 98:551–557, 1941.
6. R. S. Wallerstein and H. Sampson, "Issues in Research in the Psychoanalytic Process," *International Journal of Psychoanalysis,* 52:11–50, 1971.
7. P. L. Wachtel, *Psychoanalysis and Behavior Therapy: Toward an Integration* (New York: Basic Books), 1977.
8. J. Dollard, F. Auld, Jr., and A. White, *Steps in Psychotherapy: Study of a Case of Sex-Fear Conflict* (New York: Macmillan), 1953.
9. L. Berkowitz, "Some Determinants of Impulsive Aggression," *Psychological Review,* 81:165–174, 1974; "Aggressive Cues in Aggressive Behavior and Hostility Catharsis," Ibid., 71:102–122, 1964.
10. R. B. Stuart, "Operant-Interpersonal Treatment for Marital Discord," *Journal of Consulting and Clinical Psychology,* 33:675–682, 1969.
11. I. M. Marks, "Behavioral Treatments of Phobic and Obsessive-Compulsive Disorders: A Critical Appraisal," *Progress in Behavior Modification,* M. Hersen, R. M. Eisler, and P. M. Miller, eds. (New York: Academic Press), 1975.
12. S. W. Agras, *Panic: Facing Fears, Phobias and Anxiety* (New York: W. H. Freeman), 1985.
13. S. Benjamin, I. M. Marks, and J. Huson, "Active Muscular Relaxation in Desensitization of Phobic Patients," *Psychological Medicine,* 2:381, 1972.
14. T. D. Borkovec and J. K. Sides, "Critical Procedural Variables Related to the Physiological Effects of Progressive Relaxation: A Review," *Behavior Research and Therapy,* 17:119, 1979.
15. Agras, op. cit.
16. J. Wolpe, *Psychotherapy by Reciprocal Inhibition,* p. 216.
17. B. F. Skinner, *Walden Two* (New York: Macmillan), 1948; see also B. F. Skinner, *Science and Human Behavior* (New York: Macmillan), 1953.
18. J. G. Taylor, *The Behavioral Basis of Perception* (New Haven: Yale University Press), 1962.
19. A. T. Beck, *Cognitive Therapy and the Emotional Disorders* (New York: International Universities Press), 1976.

20. A. Ellis, *Humanistic Psychotherapy: The Rational-Emotive Approach* (New York: Julian Press), 1974.
21. M. J. Mahoney, "Reflections on the Cognitive-Learning Trend in Psychotherapy," *American Psychologist,* 32:5, 1977.
22. D. H. Meichenbaum, "Self-Instructional Methods," *Helping People Change,* F. H. Kanfer, and A. P. Goldstein, eds. (New York: Pergamon Press), 1975.
23. Beck, op. cit.
24. T. C. Wade, T. E. Malloy, and S. Proctor, "Imaginal Correlates of Self-Reported Fear and Avoidance Behavior," *Behavior Research and Therapy,* 15:17, 1977.
25. Beck, op. cit.
26. P. R. Latimer and A. A. Sweet, "Cognitive versus Behavioral Procedures in Cognitive-Behavior Therapy: A Critical Review of the Evidence," *Journal of Behavior Therapy and Experimental Psychiatry,* 1:9–22, 1984.
27. M. Biran and G. T. Wilson, "Treatment of Phobic Disorders Using Cognitive and Exposure Methods: A Self-Efficacy Analysis," *Journal of Consulting and Clinical Psychology,* 49:886–899, 1981.
28. P. M. G. Emmelkamp and P. P. Mersch, "Cognition and Exposure *In Vivo* in the Treatment of Agoraphobia: Short-Term and Delayed Effects," *Cognitive Therapy and Research,* 6:77–88, 1982.
29. See E. G. Poser, "Toward a Theory of 'Behavioral Prophylaxis,'" *Journal of Behavior Therapy and Experimental Psychiatry,* 1:45–52, 1970; M. E. Jaremko and W. W. Wenrich, "A Prophylactic Usage of Systematic Desensitization," Ibid., 4:103–105, 1973.

Special Offer

$2 discount when ordering New Harbinger Books or cassette tapes using the coupon on this page

You get **$2** off the total price when ordering from the list of books below (with a full money back guarantee). Or send for our complete catalogue of books and tapes and get the same $2 discount on orders made from the catalogue.

The Relaxation & Stress Reduction Workbook, $12.50 paperback, $22.50 hardcover

Thoughts & Feelings: The Art of Cognitive Stress Intervention, $11.50 paperback, $21.50 hardcover

Messages: The Communication Book, $10.95 paperback, $19.95 hardcover

The Divorce Book, $10.95 paperback, $19.95 hardcover

The Critical Years: A Guide for Dedicated Parents, $9.95 paperback, $19.95 hardcover

Hypnosis for Change: A Manual of Proven Hypnotic Techniques, $10.95 paperback, $20.95 hardcover

The Better Way to Drink: Moderation & Control of Problem Drinking, $10.95 paperback

The Deadly Diet: Recovering from Anorexia & Bulimia, $10.95 paperback, $19.95 hardcover

Self-Esteem, $10.95 paperback, $19.95 hardcover

Beyond Grief, $10.95 paperback, $19.95 hardcover

Chronic Pain Control Workbook, $12.50 paperback, $19.95 hardcover

Rekindling Desire, $10.95 paperback, $19.95 hardcover

Life Without Fear: Anxiety and Its Cure, $9.95 paperback, $19.95 hardcover

---

___ Please send me a free catalogue of your books and tapes. By using this coupon I will be entitled to a $2 discount on orders made from the catalogue.

___ Please send to me the following book(s). Enclosed is my check.

Price

_____ _____

_____ _____

_____

Name _____

Address _____

_____

less $2 discount	-$2.00
sales tax if Calif. res.	_____
shipping/handling	1.25
total	_____

Send to: New Harbinger Publications, Department B, 5674 Shattuck Ave., Oakland, CA 94609